# HIDDEN
# FIGURES

# HIDDEN FIGURES

## Seven Numbers Women
## Must Know for Financial Success

Linda G. Stubblefield CFP©

15151 N Frank Lloyd Wright Blvd
Scottsdale, AZ 85260

ISBN 978-1-7357-444-0-7(p)
ISBN 978-1-7357-444-1-4(e)

Library of Congress Control Number: 2020917291

Edited by Kelly Lydick—Reedsy.com
Cover art by Tim Barber----Tim@Dissectdisigns.com
Book interior and ebook design by Amit Dey—amitdey2528@gmail.com
Publishing consulting by Geoff Affleck—geoffaffleck.com

BUS027030 BUSINESS & ECONOMICS / Finance / Wealth Management
BUS050000 BUSINESS & ECONOMICS / Personal Finance / General
BUS050010 BUSINESS & ECONOMICS / Personal Finance / Budgeting
BUS050020 BUSINESS & ECONOMICS / Personal Finance / Investing
BUS050030 BUSINESS & ECONOMICS / Personal Finance / Money Management
BUS050040 BUSINESS & ECONOMICS / Personal Finance / Retirement Planning

# DEDICATION

To all those courageous, determined
women who taught me so much

# TABLE OF CONTENTS

# HOW TO USE THIS BOOK

This book will teach you seven Magic Numbers. Well, they are not *really* magic, but the **strength** and **clarification** they will bring to your financial picture are nothing short of magical. For most people, these seven numbers are Hidden. They are out of focus; distorted, and seemingly unconnected; they are forgotten or misunderstood and overlooked.

Learning these seven numbers will inform every decision you may make regarding your financial life. Learning the function of these numbers and how to balance these numbers will provide a strong foundation in your decision-making process. You will see clearly the road ahead of you and you will have more peace on the journey. Using these numbers will empower you to take control of your money… NOW.

In short, this book will show you how to:

- Understand and calculate each of the seven important figures in your life right now.
- Honestly evaluate your current financial situation.

- Bring intentionality and peace to your spending and saving habits.

- Decide what you want and need in order to create a financially secure future.

Each of these seven numbers relates to the others, and each chapter builds on the previous one. Please read them in order.

I have written an accompanying ***Hidden Figures Workbook*** that is designed to be used with your ***Hidden Figures*** book. At the end of each ***Hidden Figures*** chapter, you will want to complete corresponding "Journal" and "Worksheet" assignments in the *Workbook*. I urge you to do each of the workbook assignments before proceeding to the next chapter. The "Journal" sections will support your personal growth and introspection. The "Worksheet" sections will guide you in the discovery and calculation of your own Personal Hidden Figures.

The learning objectives written in the book will be achieved by completing the Workbook assignments. You will understand the concepts better when you put them into actions. And the Workbook will give you a consolidated space to record your discoveries and your calculations. But perhaps the most important advantage of the ***Hidden Figures Workbook*** is the access to online calculators. When you purchase the ***Hidden Figures Workbook,*** in either the print version or the electronic version, you will also be given access to online calculators. You will use the calculators and enter numbers online. One of these calculators is the Success Matrix and it is the key and culmination to learning your Hidden Figures. It is a graphic tool that will put your Hidden Figures in a new light, so you can see your total financial picture. You will use it in all your financial decisions. If you haven't already purchased the *Hidden Figures Workbook*, I urge you to do so now.

Go to: www.MyHiddenFigures.net

This process of reading, then journaling, then calculating and recording your figures will bring to life your financial growth and security plan. You will learn so much! This is a proven method of increasing your understanding and facility with new concepts. No matter what age you are, you can start on this plan today. You deserve financial growth and security. And it is never too late to create this for yourself. Never.

To be clear: This is ***not*** an investment plan. There are many books written on that very complex subject. Some are good. I've listed some of my favorites in the Resource section.

# THE UNEXPECTED LIFE

The day my mother died, she and I spent the entire morning together. It was a beautiful autumn day and we went to a quilt fair—her most favorite place on earth. We browsed beautiful patchwork in every imaginable style, color, and skill level. We admired the ribbons won by others; and those she won. She was an artisan envied by many; I was so proud of her.

We laughed, drank tea, and enjoyed the warm autumn sunshine. I drove her back to her assisted living retirement home, and she insisted I come in, so she could demonstrate to me once again how to weave handmade woolen rugs. We went through the process again and I enjoyed her passion about something for which I had no talent.

Alas, I had to go. It was time to meet with my husband and three teenage daughters. Mother and I exchanged warm hugs and soft kisses on the cheek. As I opened my car door, I heard her call one last goodbye from her patio door. She stood waiving and smiling for as long as she could see me.

If only I had known that I would never see her alive again, that I would never again hear the sound of her voice. If I had only known that those precious, memorable hours were all I would have left on this earth with her…I would have stayed, I would have said more, so much more. I would have insisted we rest more. "Why hurry through the exhibit?" "Why not have another cup of tea?" I would have…

I desperately wanted to think I could have done something to change the outcome. I searched my mind for how I might have prevented this day from coming. My heart ached, but I knew there was nothing I could have done. I had known she was ill. She had had previous strokes and heart attacks, and on that day, she had a final, massive heart attack. I unreasonably expected a different outcome. Or, at least I hadn't expected that outcome… that day.

Reality is sometimes harsh. It requires some reminding… some things are unknowable. Some things are not preventable. Events that are devastating, like my mother's death, change lives. Some things can never be the same, and we will never know which heartaches ours will be or when they will occur. All we can do is plan for possibilities.

That really is the point of financial planning. A plan does not steer us to a pristine, painless path. We have no way keep unpleasant surprises and events from happening to us, but we can create safety nets and alternate plans. We can determine reasonable expectations. And we can direct our path toward the meaningful instead of mandatory.

## Clarity About Intentions and Goals

During World War II, General Dwight D. Eisenhower said, "In preparing for battle, I have always found that plans are useless, but planning is indispensable."[1]

Making plans, re-doing plans, and making new plans is an invaluable process. Why? Because it makes us think about the things we need, want, and care about. It makes us choose, consciously, what a meaningful future looks like.

In short, planning helps us remember where we want to go. Having chosen a path, we now have a reference point so that when life pushes us off our path, we more quickly find our way back.

I have a navigation system in my car that regularly says to me, "Recalculating." What is happening? I have gotten off course, or taken a wrong turn, according to where I said I originally wanted to go. The system is figuring out where I need to go from where I am that moment.

This is an important process for all of us. Life can be confusing, but having formed a plan—a goal, a clear picture of where we want to go—makes "Recalculating" easier. This uncertain life guarantees we will have some surprises and missteps.

\*       \*       \*

[1] Nixon, Richard M., *Six Crises*, Doubleday Co., New York, New York, 1962, p. 253, quoting Gen. Dwight D. Eisenhower. This quotation is one of several versions of the statement, which was attributed by Eisenhower to "the observation of a very successful soldier who said, 'Peace-time plans are of no particular value, but peace-time planning is indispensable.'" *See also* https://quoteinvestigator.com/2017/11/18/planning/ for more variations of the theme stated in earlier times by various people from 1877 forward.

I'd like to introduce to you three women. These situations are real and did actually happen. Their names and some of the details are changed, of course, to protect their identities. Here are their stories and how they dealt with this Uncertain Life, yet used the Success Matrix to get themselves back on track.

## Mary

Mary is a highly educated, highly employable attorney. She moved across the country last year when her husband landed a plum position with a software company. In doing so, she left a lucrative position with the government in New York. After her husband had spent years being under-employed and frustrated in New York, it seemed they were finally in sync, on the same track. But the track suddenly split when Don didn't come home, and Mary was served with divorce papers. Within twelve months of the move, her husband was gone and she was suddenly on her own. Since the move, she had spent her time finding a new house and getting the family settled in their new home … not on locating a new job.

As her story tumbled out, I attempted to gather my breath and encouraged Mary to do the same. "I was really toying with staying home, since Don's job was so good, and the girls really need me while they are adjusting to new schools. They are both in private schools and are in so many clubs and extra-curricular activities … it's a full-time job just keeping up with their schedules."

"Sounds expensive, too. And now no income of your own, right? How are you taking care of the bills?" I asked.

"Well, I'm getting temporary spousal support. That will stop when the divorce settlement is reached. My eyes nearly crossed when I saw the mortgage deducted from the bank account this month."

Mary continued, "Meghan has to have a new evening gown for her sorority mixer, and Morgan's orchestra is taking a trip to Los Angeles next month. That won't be cheap, and neither will the clothes she'll want to take with her." Mary paused.

When asked about the total spending each month, Mary answered, "I really don't have a clue." She admitted that she was moving money out of the savings account each month, just to make ends meet. She ducked her head and choked back a teary sob. "I honestly can't remember what is in our account right now. Every time I start to look at our bank account, I get lost in some memory of when things were good between Don and me. And how many clues I missed months ago that he was checking out. I'm just spinning my wheels, getting nowhere."

"We'll have a lot of work to do," I warned Mary. "But I know we can get you back on track. The number one job is to find you a job." I gave her a list of things to bring for her next appointment.

## Barbara

She lost him slowly at first and then all at once. Phil was so smart. He was so financially capable. For their entire marriage, he had done everything related to finances. But one month, Barbara could see he spent all his time just shuffling papers and staring at the computer screen. Then the late bills began to arrive. A visit to the neurologist confirmed that Phil had a rare and fast-moving form of dementia. One month he was handling the finances normally. Over the next six months, he forgot all his account passwords and couldn't tell the difference between a brokerage statement and an advertising leaflet.

Barbara had left all the finances to his capable hands. She had never learned how to log into their accounts online, never read a statement, and didn't know the financial language that would allow her to communicate well with bankers or investment advisors. But she did know that their rural property in the northern Rockies was not appropriate for handling this disease. She would need to sell their current home and move closer to a major medical center for him and closer to support groups for herself. Managing the sale was one thing, but managing the new purchase and deciding what they could afford was another. She had no idea about their assets or their debts. She came to me a bundle of nerves.

I affirmed to Barbara that she was smarter than she credited herself. I assured her that she could learn everything she needed to know to make effective decisions. As the tension drained from her face, we mapped out a plan and scheduled appointments to start the process.

## Joanne

Joanne was an intelligent, active woman who enjoyed garden clubs and getaways with her grown, single daughters. She returned from one of those getaways—a yoga retreat in the desert—to find her husband dead on the floor in his home office. The shock and trauma of the event kept her in a stupor for six months. Then she awoke with a start when a letter arrived from the IRS. Not good news. The first thing I heard from Joanne was, "I don't want to learn about all this investment stuff. Just tell me what to do and if I'm going to be okay."

Although she had only talked to me once or twice before Joe's death and had never been on any of the quarterly calls with her husband, she said she totally trusted me. It wasn't easy getting her attention. I didn't know what her goals were and apparently, she didn't either, other than "to be okay."

I certainly wasn't going to proceed with an action plan when I didn't know what her objectives or long-term needs were. She didn't want to learn about the sources of the income, or the ongoing decisions that went into managing the real estate or the investment portfolio or the tax obligations of each. I knew she had no idea what she owned and, more importantly, she didn't know some basic money management principles to help her make decisions about her future. I was glad to be her advisor, but I needed her active participation and willingness to learn. I suspected she was simply afraid to admit what she didn't know.

I rarely hear those attitudes spoken these days: "Let someone else take care of it." More often I find couples are dividing up financial responsibilities or each is managing his/her own portfolio. I hear women saying they want to be involved, more competent in their finances. Whether they are married or not, have a partner or not, they are taking on the responsibility. Gradually, Joanne realized that she was just too vulnerable if she didn't take more responsibility herself. She dug in and did the work with me to educate herself and understand the pros and cons of each of her financial decisions.

## Who are you?

Throughout my career, a great many of my clients have been women, usually divorced or widowed, "Suddenly Single." I have walked with them through these painful eras of their lives. I have taught them how to take full responsibility for their own financial well-being during incredibly stressful times, when they had little to no preparation. I taught them how to think financially and make good decisions for themselves, even though they often called, saying, "I don't know what I am doing!" I taught them how to calmly use appropriate financial tools to resolve their challenges in an empowering way.

I showed them that they can and must step up to the plate. It has been a rewarding career teaching woman seven numbers—the Hidden Figures—in their financial life; the meaning of those numbers, and how to use them to their advantage. I have seen firsthand that once they have the Hidden Figures numbers mastered, their financial decision-making quotient jumps sky high. They have the confidence to sit in the driver's seat, steering their own lives in the right direction, choosing with excitement the path before them.

That is who I am writing for: the suddenly single who are new to financial management. I am empowering people who want to competently manage their money in this unexpected life.

*In 1950, unmarried citizens represented only 33% of the adult population in the United States. ("Unmarried" includes never married, separated, divorced, and widowed.) By 2011, the US Census Bureau reported that married couples represented only 48% - a sharp drop of 19%. By 2014, the US Bureau of Labor Statistics reported that 124.6 million Americans 16 years and above were "unmarried." That is, roughly 51% of our citizens were unmarried as compared with 33% in 1950 and 37.4% as late as 1976. 2018 US Census Bureau statistics show another 1.3% drop in married adults over a span of four years. The huge growth in the unmarried adults from 1950 to 2018 is largely – 53.7% – women.*[2]

2   https://www.csmonitor.com/USA/Society/2015/0614/Singles-nation-Why-so-many-Americans-are-unmarried. *See also* https://data.census.gov/cedsci/table?

## Journal Assignment

I encourage you to take some quiet time at the end of each chapter to write about what you just read. There are two sides to money management. One is driven by logical, executive decisions. The other is driven by our emotions and baggage from the past.

I'm no psychologist and I'm not trying to offer therapy here. But I find when we write while in a rested, objective state, a new awareness can emerge. A wisdom we didn't know was there often comes into play and deposits beautiful clarity right in our laps. We can learn things from our inner wisdom that we hadn't previously known was there. Skip over to your Workbook (www.MyHiddenFigures.net) now to read the journal prompts. Then open your journal notebook and write!

# PART I

# SEVEN HIDDEN FIGURES

# INCOME

When my client, Mary, returned the next week, she was bubbling about her new job with a large estate planning firm. "They offered a salary plus a percentage of my billable hours," she said with satisfaction, a huge weight clearly lifted from her shoulders.

"Oh, very good!" I applauded. But when we moved to discussing the hard numbers, things got slippery. "You mean you agreed to work, but you don't know how much salary you'll be paid?" I asked.

Mary scrunched up her face. She was desperate to feel safe again. Clearly, she had made some progress in landing a good job. But she had stepped into one of those pitfalls common to women: she had taken a job without asking her new employer for a firm salary commitment. I am amazed at how often this happens. Maybe it has happened to you. You were so happy to have the job, you were afraid to ask how much the pay was. You feared the question might sound crass or greedy. You thought the job was such a good opportunity that you didn't consider that you were also a good opportunity for the firm.

In other words, you were afraid the hiring manager would not confirm your worth.

A crucial part of your financial plan is *clarity*. When I ask a new client for her income, and she says, "Oh, I'm not sure. It's around 80 something …," I know we have work to do. Here's why: If you don't know your income - how much money is coming in - then I promise you, you don't know how much money is going out. And you are not clear about your monetary worth.

When you are agreeing on employment or a new position, despite your biggest fears, you must not be afraid to ask for the hard numbers and negotiate what is fair. Being clear is paramount to being safe. Standing up for yourself is paramount to being safe.

More about your worth later...

## Your Income

If you work a job, you should know your Gross Salary. That's *not* your take-home pay. If you are married, you should know your individual and your joint Gross Income. If you have a job with variable income, you should know your Average Gross Income. If you are retired, you should know the numbers that make up your retirement income, even if from various sources, as a Gross Income. No worries. I'm going to help you sort this out, if you are not already there.

First, let's understand the difference in Gross Income (or salary) and Net Income (or salary). "Gross" means your pay before anything is taken out for taxes. "Net" Income is the amount of your income after subtracting taxes. Both of those numbers have significance. But for now, we will only need your Gross Income.

Let's identify the sources of your income. That information will affect many other things down the road.

## Employment Wages

Are you an employee? If you have a salary, or wages, from an employer who withholds taxes for you, you are an employee. That makes things simple. Find your most recent paystub. Find the *gross* pay. Multiply that number times the number of times you get paid in a year. If you get paid once a month, multiply times 12. If you get paid twice a month, multiply times 24. If you get paid every two weeks, multiply times 26. And if you get paid weekly, multiply times 52. It's that easy. That's your Annual Gross Income.

## Overtime or Bonuses

Some people get paid overtime. If that is you, ask if it is a regular thing or just a once in a while thing. If you are consistently getting paid overtime, then you can count it as part of your Annual Gross Income. Multiply the average overtime you are paid by the number of times you get paid overtime in a year, and add it to your Annual Gross Salary. The total is your Annual Gross Income.

If you are like most people, who only get overtime pay in special circumstances, then count this as bonus income. It should be saved during the year or set aside for special use, but not counted on or used for regular expenses. Or maybe you are paid a bonus once a year. Bonuses generally fluctuate. Again, that is not the figure we are searching for here. We want the *amount that you can regularly depend on*; a number that is safe to use in determining what you can afford and cannot afford. As an employee, a W-2 wage earner, your taxes will also be withheld from the bonuses and overtime. Make sure you are using the gross, before taxes are withheld.

## Commission or Mostly-Commission Person

Many people have income that is irregular and fluctuates from month to month. Many commission-based workers (realtors, for instance) have significant income that comes infrequently and/or sporadically. Because your income may vary greatly from month to month and year to year, you have some special budgeting needs. You will have to come up with the most conservative average of your last few years. You may be paid purely on a productivity scale, or perhaps you earn a small salary, and the commissions are paid on top of that.

In any case, if any part of your income is commissions, your income is irregular. You have a little project.

1. Locate the most recent 3 months income. We are looking for Annual Gross Income (before taxes are taken out). In other words, you'll total the last three months earnings, divide by 3 and multiply by 12 to get an average Annual Gross amount from the most recent quarter.

2. Now get a total in all income from the last 12 months. The total of this income, before taxes were deducted, is your Gross Income for the last 12 months.

3. Now find your total Annual Gross Income for the last 3 years, (found on your 1099 or your last paycheck stubs for each of the last three years). Divide this number by three.

You have a judgment call on this one. By looking at all three numbers, you can analyze your income. Here are some questions you should ask yourself:

- How much did these numbers fluctuate from month to month and year to year?
- Does the annualized income for the last three months closely match my last 12 months' income?
- Does my last 12 months' income closely match my average for the last 3 years?
- Is there some predictability? Or are there seasonal swings in the income?
- Is there a steady increase over the last three years? Or does the trend look erratic or decreasing?

What number you use in the Annual Gross Income is your decision. It must be an estimate that helps you stay within safety guidelines on your spending. In a later chapter, we will deal with how to manage that fluctuation. For now, just reach a comfortable agreement with yourself about how much income you can dependably count on. The Gross Income you use in your worksheet is an estimate that will be useable in making plans if things stay as they are. Knowing what you made in recent months and years will help determine what is reasonably relied upon this year. Adjust according to what feels safe for you.

And remember, this is **not** an income goal. Go ahead, set a very high goal. Dream away. Reach for the stars. But the Income you put into your Success Matrix is *a number you can depend on*, that will keep you thinking straight about what is affordable and wise for you. If you hit your goal and make 100% more than you entered on your Success Matrix, you will have some very happy planning to do. If the opposite happens, your income is 100% less than you were planning on, it won't be so fun.

## Self-Employment

If you get a 1099 from your employer at the end of the year, and no taxes have been withheld from your checks, you are a 1099 worker. As a self-employed or contract worker, you are most likely responsible for some or all of your business expenses: equipment, supplies, marketing, travel, research, *etc*. A true business owner has an extra step for calculating Gross Income. Depending on how you are legally organized—as a sole proprietor or S Corp or a C Corp—the taxes may be figured differently.

For now, all we're trying to come up with is a number that you can use to make your personal spending budget. Your Hidden Figure for income is never going to be the same from year to year. To plan for your fluctuating income, follow the instructions above for the Commission or Mostly Commission person. Everything said to the Commission person applies to you, too. Once you have that average number written down, you will need to subtract your **business expenses.** Your revenue minus expenses—that is *your* Gross Income. That is what you will report to the IRS as your income. That number is used to enter in your Success Matrix.

## Retirement Income

If you are retired, you probably have income coming from several different sources. Maybe you have Social Security. And you may also have a pension. Then there may be some investment income. Your Hidden Figure for income includes all of these sources. However, the investment income most likely fluctuates. Calculate, first, all guaranteed income: Social Security, pensions or annuities. That is one number to know for sure. Then calculate your investment income with an eye to what could change in the future. Be conservative in your estimate. Know if the investment income you are counting on liquidates some of your investment principal or if it is pure dividend and interest. If you don't know, it is time to talk with your investment advisor. You should be *very clear* on this part. In any case, your income is the total of all your income sources that is safe to depend upon year after year. Reading the rationale given in the Commissions section will also help you come to a reasonable income number for your Success Matrix.

## Rental or Real Estate Income

Income from real estate will come under the same rules as Self-Employment. Your income comes with some expenses. And if you are not paying any expenses right now, you may in the future, so you should be putting some of your income aside to pay for those upcoming expenses (repairs, months without renters, finding renters, insurance, *etc.*). Please calculate your income, and deduct the potential or known expenses. Look at your *gross* personal income from real estate as the net after expenses. This is what you must budget and work with. You, too, should read the Commissions section.

## Combinations

Maybe you have a combination of these situations. You may have an employer but also run a business in your off hours.

You may be retired, but also have a rental property, or a consulting business that cash flows and gives you income. There are many combinations and all of them work. Enter the separate sources of income on separate lines.

## Guaranteed Income

Be clear on how much income is guaranteed. Guaranteed income is that which is backed by the government or a company and promised for your lifetime or a certain period. This would include Social Security or pensions or annuities. These payments are not dependent on the stock market or the hiring whims of a company. Guaranteed income is entered on a separate line in your Success Matrix.

### The Feminine Perspective on Income

A woman's income needs are not really any different from a man's. Both groups need sufficient income to last a lifetime. That income usually comes from a combination of Social Security income and a stockpile of retirement savings. Since, statistically speaking, women typically live longer than men, either their Social Security check needs to be sufficient or their retirement savings bigger. Here's where an interesting twist of Social Security law enters the calculus and calls for some extra consideration.

Social Security **lifetime** benefits (as distinguished from Social Security **death** benefits) are calculated based on the thirty-five (35) highest earning years before age 60. After age 60, your earnings are not indexed for inflation. Therefore, your late-career earnings are *not* increased like your early-career earnings.

What does this mean for many women? They often sacrifice their early careers for the family. For example, they may not work at all during child-bearing and child-rearing years. They may also take lower-paying jobs or a less-challenging (and thus, lower-compensation) career path to support their spouse's career moves. They are also more likely than men to take family leave time for sick children or parents. All of this is good for the family. But it has the effect of penalizing the woman in her Social Security benefits.

If she is currently married (or in the case of divorce, was married for at least 10 years), then she has a choice, for **lifetime** benefits (*i.e.*, an affirmative election must be made by her to the Social Security Administration) of taking 100% of her own earned benefit **or** one-half ($\frac{1}{2}$) of her husband's or ex-husband's earned benefit (for her, called the Social Security Spousal Benefit). It's important to note that this is an election between 100% of her own benefit or $\frac{1}{2}$ of her husband's—not both. (No, it does **not** reduce the husband's benefit at all.)

And equally important, the wife's election is *not* a permanent election; it can be changed. For example, if you were born before 1954, you are allowed to take the spousal benefit for a while, letting your own earned benefit grow to maximum, and then switch to your benefit amount. The point is that you need to be aware of the spousal benefit rules; otherwise, you may pay dearly in the long run with a smaller Social Security check caused by the potential earnings lost on behalf of the family during child-bearing and rearing years.

Then, of course, there is the problem of lower wages. If women earn lower wages during their careers, because they don't stand up for themselves, or they are unfairly limited to lower wages, or they have sacrificed time in the workplace that would give them seniority in their positions, then it clearly follows that their individual savings rates in retirement accounts would be smaller, as well. All 401(k) contributions are based on a percentage of your salary, both the employee's contributions and the employer's match. Smaller wages equal smaller contributions from both.

Women need to consider this throughout their career and earning years. Women in their 30s and 40s should wise up to these facts that will affect them mightily in their retirement years. Old age is not inexpensive.

When Mary accepted the position in the law firm without clarifying the salary, she may as well have slipped the managing partner a note that read, "You can take advantage of me. I will not complain." When women know they are being passed over for raises and promotions and say nothing, they are acquiescing to a bleaker future as an 80-year-old, and they should acknowledge their choice. Every financial advisor agrees that the most oft-expressed fears from a pre-retiree are, "I don't want to be a burden on my children" and "I'm afraid I'll run out of money." Specifically, from women, I hear, "I don't want to be a bag lady."

Here's the point: The time is *now* to be clear about your money. Know your income now. Educate yourself about your worth and your career potential. Acknowledge the events that could derail you in your quest for financial security and plan a way around the pitfalls. It's part of being in integrity with yourself. That's what knowing your income can do for you.

## Integrity and Stewardship

Acknowledging keeps you in integrity with yourself, who you are and what your intentions are. Planning for your income is the first step in taking responsibility for that money. Stewardship comes to mind. What is stewardship? It is taking care of and taking responsibility for something or someone. You have been awarded a certain amount of money to manage. Be it little or a lot, no one else will manage it to your exact goals but you. The first step of accepting that responsibility is to acknowledge the annual dollar amount. Ask yourself, "Can I take pride in the number?" Will you promise yourself you will take good care of it? Can you embrace all of your feelings around this important hidden figure: Your Income?

### There are Workbook assignments awaiting you

Turn to your Income workbook pages. You'll find Journal Prompts in the Journal Section. And Worksheets are in the Worksheet Section. Complete them before going to the next chapter. If you have not purchased the Workbook, do so now. (www.MyHiddenFigures.net)

# SPENDING

Your expenses include your spending, your debt payments, and your taxes. This chapter is about your spending. We want to get as clear on that number as we got on your income. Later, we'll drill down into the debt payments and taxes. Then we will discuss and analyze how much you *can* spend. Today, let's find the real number of how much you *do* spend. The truth is: **you will never be safe financially until you spend less than you earn.**

You can only do two things with your income: Spend it or save it. That's it. You are either trading your money for stuff and experiences or you are saving it. If you are saving your money, you are simply putting it in another pocket, to spend another day. When my clients say they are not sure how much they are spending, I respond, "That's easy. Calculate your contributions to the 401(k), and your increased balance in your savings accounts. Everything else, you spent.

Mary, wanted to quibble. Her divorce had been finalized. She got the house, along with the huge mortgage, and half of the retirement and investment accounts. She was awarded no alimony, since she had a good career and income closely equal to her ex-spouse. They agreed to split the expenses for the two teenagers.

Now we were moving ahead with building her Success Matrix and she didn't like my calculations of how much money she was spending. "But I save $1,600 out of my paycheck every month!"

"Really? Tell me about that."

"I put $800 in my 401(k) and transfer $800 to my bank savings account every month!"

"That would mean for six months, you've added $800 to the savings account. Well, then you should have about $4,800 more in your savings account than you did six months ago. Do you?"

"Well, no." She said. "I had to buy some furniture this year after the divorce. Don took a lot of furniture from the house to furnish his new apartment."

"Fine. Then how much is in the savings account compared to last year?" I asked.

"There isn't anything in the savings account," Mary admitted. "I spent it all on stuff I needed for the house."

Right. The key word is "spent." Even if you are adding money to the savings account, if you spend any part of it, you must acknowledge that amount in your expenses and deduct it from your savings.

I added, "Bravo for not using a credit card. You had savings set aside and you used it instead of your credit card. That was really good. But," I continued, "whatever you take out of the account goes in the Expense column. You spent it."

To calculate Mary's spending, we looked at her paycheck. We took her gross salary, subtracted the 401(k) contributions and taxes. The difference was how much she was spending.

Back to my original premise: You are either spending your money or saving it. Know which one you are doing. Don't call it by another name. Remember when I said, "Show me someone who doesn't know how much she earns and I will show you someone who doesn't know how much she spends." It's true, isn't it?

I usually avoid sports analogies. In fact, I hate them. But last year during the Super Bowl game—the one game I watch all year—it hit me. The commentators in the broadcast booth were talking about three different parts of the game. There was the "head game"—the analysis of the players' attitudes or their conflicted thinking. Perhaps one player might have a personal vendetta against another player; maybe one had an injury that could make him or her hesitant; or maybe there was a personal problem that could interfere with the player's focus. The commentators discussed the pressures, the past failures, the team's determination, or the likelihood of giving up. That's the head game.

Then there is the play on the field—the actual game is the second part.

After particular plays, however, the commentators often showed instant replays. Those instant replays plus the entire game films made by each team are the third part. Reviewing those films and instant replays enables us to see what must change in order to succeed. The players and coaches and referees have to see the actual play, not just in mind or memory. It must be viewed in "black and white," so to speak. That's how

they learn what *really* happened on the field. That's how players, coaches, and referees spot and correct mistakes.

Every athlete knows the importance of the head game, the
game on the field, and the game films and instant replays. The
game on the field is never great if the head game is a mess.
The game on the field always requires one's best, slacking will
not bring a win. And the study of the replays and game films
actually has a big potential impact on the next game. The
replays and game films must be studied as a learning source.
They all work together.

That is how we need to learn about our spending. We need
to analyze the head game that is ruling our thoughts about
our spending. Those thoughts might be the basis of a lot of
our spending actions. We also must require our own personal
"best" when we're in shopping mode: online, in the stores, and
out with friends. The replay is in looking at how the money has
been spent in the past. it is analyzing the patterns and actually
calculating the amounts spent. That's the replay. That's where
you get better. Let's take a closer look at each part.

## The Head Game

Consumer advertising is designed to make us spend. Its success is measured in clicks of the mouse and customers in the
store and most of all: dollars spent. We are told repeatedly that
some things are priceless, and you can use your credit card to
have those priceless things. Target Stores advertise their goods
with a picture of a heart. In other words, "You love this stuff
and you know it." Online ads for clothing show that more is
better than less. Shopping for sparkly new things is fun and
brings relief from a humdrum life or a painful life. We are

told that to be rich, we have to have lots of stuff and that rich people have more fun…with all their stuff.

The only way around this life of consumerism is to recognize the real, true value of our lives, the value of our loved ones, beauty, rest, a clear conscience…and so many other things. Once gratitude and appreciation set in, we can see all around us the bounty of free things in life. I suggest you read *The Millionaire Next Door* by Thomas J. Stanley. See that not all millionaires want more and more stuff. We need to quit believing the advertising messages. If you have a real problem with overspending, to stay out of the stores and stop reading catalogs. Make a game of seeing how much money you can keep in your wallet. See spending in an entirely new way.

Interestingly, it is just as important to look at *scarcity* beliefs. I have battled a "scarcity" mindset most of my life. It is a subconscious belief that there won't be enough. ("Maybe others have enough, but not me," you might say.) That mindset is a plague and I believe it keeps us from receiving all that is available to us in very tangible ways. It can trigger greed and/or hoarding. Seeing the world with either scarcity or abundance is a state of mind that we choose. You can have either mindset with virtually any set of circumstances in your life. It is up to you to observe this subconscious belief and choose differently.

I encourage you to look honestly at your attitudes toward money and spending. Your spending habits are a reflection of how you think about money. If you are having trouble with your spending, pulling back the cover on your attitudes will help. I have supplied some thought-provoking ideas in the journal. I encourage you to spend some time in reflection. Get to the heart of your thoughts and you will better control your actions.

## Game On

Your goal for this chapter is to track what you are spending. Study your spending instant replay! You need to look back and see exactly where and how much you are spending right now. You will set up the spending **plan** or **budget** (what you want to spend in each category) in the Cash Flow chapter. Don't worry about that now.

Spending is divided in two major categories: **Essential spending** and **Non-Essential spending**. What is essential to your survival is: food, housing, transportation, health care, and insurance. Non-Essential spending is everything else. You must understand anything *not* essential to your survival is a luxury.

Seeing both of these categories is a must to understanding your spending world. Admittedly, you have huge leeway in deciding how much is "needed." Each of us decides how much we will spend on food. We know we have to have food. Some spend a little, some are extravagant. Regarding housing, some sort of housing is essential, but you are allowed to choose whether you rent a room in someone else's home or purchase a house in San Francisco. Food, housing, transportation, health care, and insurance are each Essential, but how much you spend in each category is up to you. When we put together a spending plan, you can decide if you are spending too much or too little. For now, let's just discover what your spending habits are.

## Food

What does it take to nourish your body? I take this very seriously. Nourishing food is essential. And what I spend on frozen yogurt or specialty coffees does not count. Those are luxuries. I can't go into nutrition here, but your body certainly requires nutrients to live. I encourage you to make feeding your body healthy foods a priority, so that your body flourishes. Learn to do well by your body. The great thing is that top quality fruits and vegetables are much less expensive than manufactured food and satisfy you more.

## Housing

If you rent, your rent payment is included in this figure. If you have purchased a home using a mortgage, then include the mortgage payment in your Essential Spending. Find out if your mortgage payment includes taxes and insurance. If they are **not** included, add your real estate taxes. (Your homeowners' insurance can be added here or in the Insurance section, just don't enter it twice.) Also include HOA dues and average annual repairs/upkeep for the house. Now, add all utility payments. Do *not* include furnishing the house in these essential costs. That is a choice and it goes with the Non-Essential Spending.

## Transportation

You may drive a Mercedes Benz or a Chevy Vibe; you may use Uber, rent a car, or use the bus or subway. Whatever your transportation choices are, be sure you include gasoline, licenses, tolls, parking, maintenance and repairs, as appropriate, for any mode of transportation you own, lease or rent. Include the cost of replacing tires periodically, as well as periodic maintenance for such items as a radiator flush and antifreeze/coolant, *etc*. And just as in the housing category, if you have a car loan, the payment is included in the Essential Spending category.

## Health Care

We spend money on our health in one way or another. I prefer to spend money on excellent, nutritious food and vitamins and preventive care. When calculating health care, first calculate your out-of-pocket expenses for doctors and prescriptions. Look at the past couple of years and average that amount. However, if you are retired, I encourage you to use your insurer's annual out-of-pocket maximum in the calculations. Also include non-covered treatments that you believe enhance your health, like vitamins, chiropractors, acupuncturists and other treatments you may utilize from time to time. I choose to cut back in other areas of spending so these things are affordable for me. You get to choose what is important to you.

## Insurance

Why is insurance included in Essential Spending, you may ask? Insurance is a cost-spreading mechanism to make the out-of-pocket costs for a large item affordable for everyone who participates in the large population of insured parties. In other words, it's cheaper for me to insure my home for a couple thousand dollars per year than to replace the whole value if it burns down. I cannot save enough money quickly enough to always be able to replace my home, my car, etc.

In this day and time, with growing risks and costs for health care, and lawsuits and/or accidents, insurance is a necessary part of our lives. We buy insurance to cover a cost that we cannot afford to pay outright. For instance, trying to replace a house lost to fire or storm would most likely ruin you financially. Whatever you cannot afford to replace from your own pocket, you should insure within reasonable limits. Life insurance replaces your income at your death for those who are dependent upon your income. Home or renters' insurance, auto insurance, health insurance, and liability insurance replace assets or reimburse costs for unexpected catastrophic losses.

For each of these essential spending categories, record how much you spend annually.

## Non-Essential Spending

Debt and Taxes are expenses with their own categories and will be covered in later chapters. Non-Essential Spending includes everything else you want to have or do: Electronic and live entertainment, travel, clothes, shopping of all kinds, costs related to fitness, *etc*. Don't gasp and tell me these are essential. You can walk outside for free. You can do calisthenics or pushups, ab crunches and yoga in your own home, for free. Whether you do or not is up to you – it's your decision.

I doubt you will go naked if you don't buy new clothes for this year or next. And yes, we all need relaxation time. But that could be a picnic. You could take a siesta on the porch. Whatever you spend in this category is LUXURY. You can get along without it. If you can afford it – Great! There's no problem. Let's just be clear about the *necessity* of it.

## Handling Emergencies

Congratulations on the decision to get your financial life in order! But you're not there yet. There are emergencies that may pop up. If you are confronted with having $58 in your account and $600 worth of bills yet to be paid, I want you to have a checklist.

First, *get your head in order*. Re-read "Head Game" above. Notice what you have been saying or thinking that put you into the problem that now confronts you. What you say to yourself in these situations *really does* matter. You can berate yourself for being a stupid idiot. You can complain about life and declare, "I'll never get ahead!" Nothing ever works out for me!" Or you can look at reality, acknowledge mistakes that were made, and see things you need to change in order to avoid repeating this situation. In other words, you take responsibility and control. Then decide what has to be done to remedy the situation. In this way, you are supporting change in your life. You are constructively managing your way out.

In the game on the field, there are only 3 things you can do:

- Bring in more money
  - ○ Work overtime
  - ○ Sell something
  - ○ Earn a commission
- Spend less
  - ○ Decide that you can survive on what you have for the rest of the month.
  - ○ Only spend on necessities—food and gasoline.

○ Delay paying bills until the end of the month or until next month, if possible. Contact the payees to let them know your plans. This may avoid a collection action against you.

○ Pay ½ of bills due for anything that is flexible, or negotiate a longer payment schedule.

- Use Emergency Savings or Credit

  ○ This, of course, assumes you have savings or credit available.

  ○ If you do have either, and you opt to use it, you should set aside extra money in the future to pay it back (plus the interest if you used credit).

  ○ This should be the last resort.

  ○ If this is your first response, re-read the previous pages.

Throughout this process, overcome the panic by journaling and becoming reflective, not condemning. Assess what can be done. Do what is reasonable. There is only the present. Live in the present.

## Keeping Track

When you complete the Workbook exercises, you will see exactly how much and where you are spending. If you are not already using some sort of electronic bookkeeping system, some way to track your spending, you may want to start one now. I recommend it. You could be spending from several different sources: checking accounts, payroll deductions, credit cards, savings accounts and brokerage accounts are the most likely suspects. You don't want to have to search and add everything each month or quarter. The electronic systems will keep you from having to do that.

There are many ways to accomplish this. Please refer to the Resource pages for some ideas on electronic apps for bookkeeping. Your bank may have what you need. Whether you purchase an app or use something free from your bank, it doesn't matter. It's the doing it, tracking it, *and spending time analyzing* it that really matters. You are being accountable to yourself. And accountable to your dreams.

Complete the assignments in your Spending chapter of the Workbook. (Purchase the Workbook here: www.MyHiddenFigures. net) Once you have totaled your Essential Spending and your Non-Essential Spending, you will have completed perhaps the most crucial and difficult of the Hidden Figures. This is incredibly important to your financial health. You really are on your way! I hope you are appreciating your own progress!

# DEBT

*I* have a secret; a past. Like everyone else, I have made financial mistakes. The biggest of them haunts me. But I have learned to leverage that mistake into personal growth. As a financial planner, I somehow thought the rules didn't apply to me, that I could somehow outsmart "the system." I used debt ("leverage," they euphemistically call it) and I brought my financial house down around my ears.

My net worth was just over one million. I was in the last quarter of my career. The stock market and the real estate market had moved higher and higher, a seemingly endless progression. In contrast to my advice to clients, I acted like it would never end. I used all my emergency funds and pledged my assets to buy a brand-new "can't lose" investment property in a large metropolitan area.

I knew that if it worked, it would be beautiful. And I had every confidence it *would* work. The cash flow would pay for the mortgage, the mortgage would pay down the debt, and together with the rising real estate market, I would create a

profitable asset, which I could sell and buy a financial planning firm. Beautiful plan.

It should have worked. But it didn't. The economy started
tanking. Jobs were being lost, plants closing, and whole industries
were shutting down. My lessees didn't renew their lease because
their businesses had dried up. With three major firms and an area
military base closing, there were no new lessees to be found. The
supply was much greater than the demand. As the real estate
market, especially commercial real estate, sank lower and lower, I
not only couldn't find renters; I couldn't find a buyer for the property either. It was no longer a cash-flowing property in a prosper-
ous community. It was no longer a saleable property.

The stock market dropped 50%. As a result, the boutique
financial planning firm that had hired me as Senior Planner,
the one I was planning to buy in two short years, panicked
with their own financial losses. They no longer could afford a
Senior Planner. They eliminated my job and ultimately closed
their doors.

Next was the accident. I got a call from my husband's
phone, but it wasn't my husband on the other end. One of
my husband's cycling friends spoke with a shaky voice, telling me to be calm. I learned Michael had been injured and
was headed to the nearest emergency room, probably facing
surgery. In the next days and weeks, we faced the possibility
that he might not ever walk again. This began the multitude
of decisions to arrange life for his healing and recovery. My
husband was, and still is a strong, determined individual. In
time, he did recover and for that we are so grateful.

That didn't change the fact, however, that we had soar-
ing medical bills from his surgery and physical therapy that

were only partially covered by insurance. I had no job and our investment property that was supposed to be paying for itself was now demanding mortgage payments.

Michael was now off work for three months with short-term disability paying only 2/3 of his salary. Trying to keep afloat was like trying to put out a housefire with a beach bucket. We were spending our savings at an alarming rate. Eventually, the banks foreclosed on almost a million dollars in real estate, including our home, and we were forced into bankruptcy. It was the proverbial "bad day at Black Rock."

I thought it would destroy me, especially if people knew. I wanted to keep everything private. But in my industry, there is no such thing. I had to disclose the bankruptcy to the boards and agencies that govern my industry. It took all my courage and faith just to choke back the tears and keep going.

## Think About It

What was obviously a bad move in hindsight, seemed reasonable and prudent at the time. I took calculated risks because I was hopeful, enthusiastic, optimistic. I had high goals. I believed in myself. I thought luck, or God, or talent was on my side. And I wanted to do something meaningful with my life. All good intentions, right?

Maybe you have had a similar experience from the global meltdown of 2008 or before. Millions did. For me, it turned out, the risks I took were not well calculated. No one can calculate the future, much less predict the Great Recession. But I failed to take into my calculations that economies change and jobs can disappear. I didn't have a Plan B for those eventualities.

This chapter is about debt. There is no other financial decision you can make that will put you in more peril than debt. This chapter will challenge your pre-conceived notions about debt, will de-bunk the "conventional wisdom" spouted about debt and hopefully change your financial life for the better. We will help you set up guardrails in your finances. We accept the Unpredictability; the Unexpectedness of Life; and we plan for possible eventualities. We will make decisions regarding debt that will not put your financial future at risk. *"Plan for the worst, hope for the best,"* says the old axiom.[3]

Facing my mistakes, admitting them and making agreements with myself brought the healing and correction I needed. I also wrote my "Safety Rules" that would keep me from ever making those mistakes again. I'll share those later. For now, let's explore why we get in debt in the first place.

## The Heavy Cost of Debt

Some people get into debt to make money. Others are trying to impress or fill a void. But all debt comes from wanting something you can't afford or don't want to pay for on your own.

I recently watched the movie *Madame Bovary*, a 2015 movie production of a nineteenth-century novel by Gustave Flaubert. Madame Emma Bovary was the heroine of a story about the rising middle class. Poor Emma was bored and she was naive. She craved acceptance and excitement. Then a

---

3 A common saying that pretty much everyone agrees on. Maya Angelou wrote in *I Know Why the Caged Bird Sings*, "Hoping for the best, prepared for the worst, and unsurprised by anything in between." Zig Ziglar said, "Expect the best. Prepare for the worst. Capitalize on what comes." Denis Waitley said, "Expect the best, plan for the worst, and prepare to be surprised."

traveling merchant brought goods to her home, excited her desire to have more and be more. He said the most enchanting things to her. "You don't have to pay for it," he purred. "I can give you the money … on credit … You can pay me whenever you like." He flaunted beautiful fabrics, showed her what a new Persian rug would do for her living room, and put a beautiful candelabra on her table top. "Money should never stand in the way of having the things you love," he deceptively assured her.

Madame Bovary filled her house with beautiful furnishings and her closet with exquisite clothing. Her debt was just as stunning. She built up 10,000 French francs in debt, a devastating amount in the mid-1800s. When she attempted to pay her tab, her debt collector was described as "more ferocious than a bear." The heavy gold candelabra and beautiful shell cutlery offered to the lender—items she felt were priceless—didn't scratch the surface in reducing her debt. Devasted, Emma added her jewelry to the offering, which she treasured even more. But the resale value was still far short of the debt. She and her prominent husband were bankrupt.

Most of us recognize Emma's temptation, which plays out in the boutiques and malls or online for us. We've played it ourselves. The things that seem incredibly necessary in the moment are soon lost, discarded, forgotten, even despised when the pain of payment stares us in the face.

We give up our financial security, our peace of mind, and sometimes even our reputation and relationships for these things. We tell ourselves that we cannot do without them, that this is a once-in-a-lifetime opportunity. Yet when they bring us pain, we would throw them out in a heartbeat just to have a semblance of the peace and security we threw away on impulse.

That's the high price of debt. "The rich rule over the poor, and the borrower is slave to the lender," says Proverbs 22:7 (NIV). In other words, the cost of debt is slavery.

## Different Kinds Of Debt?

I hear it all the time. "All debt isn't bad, is it? Isn't there such a thing as good debt?" If we take it out of the "good and bad" realm, I think we can analyze and agree that there are reasonable ways to use debt. The primary questions are these:

- Are you buying an appreciating asset, a depreciating asset, or a disappearing asset?
- And do you have a Plan A and Plan B to pay for the debt?

### Appreciating Assets

If you purchase an item, an asset, and that item will increase in value over time, you can call it an Appreciating Asset (AA). As a general rule, I would say that it is reasonable to borrow money for the appreciating asset. Take for instance, the mortgage on your house. You purchase (with borrowed money) a home with a market value of $200,000. In 20 years, it is worth $450,000 and your debt is nearly paid off. The home is an appreciating asset. On average, the house will go up in value 4% each year. Over time, the item you borrowed so many thousands of dollars for, may be worth more than what you paid for it. But that is no hard and fast guarantee. Property values can tumble in unexpected ways and in perilous times. Keep your eyes wide open.

There aren't too many other instances where you can borrow for an appreciating asset and have it make sense. For instance, you can borrow for stock purchases. That's called buying on margin, and by doing so, you have just increased your risk by 50%! Few people have the skillset to manage the risk of stock plus an additional 50% risk. You also could purchase art or jewelry on credit. These, in theory, will appreciate. But tastes in jewelry and art may skid with current styles, and with it goes their market value. Finding the right buyer may also prove difficult. These items are definitely a long-term hold. If you are buying on credit, it simply means you pay a higher price (purchase price plus interest). Always calculate the total interest paid over the term of the loan and add it to your purchase price to see if it is still a reasonable investment.

Sometimes, people put the AA tag on education. I can see where they come from on that score. If you have a job promised to you with that degree or certification, sometimes it makes sense to accept a loan. For instance, if you are making $30,000 a year and your income will jump $50,000 a year or more, a $30,000 loan would make sense. You can use the increased income to pay off the loan in two years or so, and as long as the job is secure, I would say it is worth it. But it takes some careful calculations to make sure you are not looking at this through a rose-colored lens. Still, in general, you could say that education is an appreciating asset. Again, calculate the total interest paid over the term of the loan and add it to your purchase price. Does it still make sense to borrow for this education?

Anytime you take a loan, the lending merchant should give you an amortization table, showing the rate at which you will pay down the principle. You should also get a total for the interest paid over the term of the loan. Ask for this if it is not readily given. Always! Do not sign without it.

## Depreciating Assets

A depreciating asset is just what you might think it is. An appreciating asset goes up in value over time; a depreciating asset loses its value over time. Take your car, for instance. A new car depreciates at least 10% when you drive it off the lot. It also depreciates approximately 10% every year thereafter. So, you might buy a car for $30,000 with a down payment of $5,000 and a loan for the balance of $25,000. That gives you equity (market value minus loan value) of $5,000. By the next year, your car value is reduced to $24,300 and the loan has dropped to $29,400. What is your new equity? Negative $5,100! That is a depreciating asset, and the math is obvious. You have lost ground.

Furniture is another example of a depreciating assets, as is designer clothing. These items have some resale value. But really very little and nothing compared to their depreciation rate!

In my opinion, it is a bad idea to borrow for these items. Use debt for such purposes only if cash flow is good but your assets are too low to pay for the item and the item is essential. (Maybe you got kicked out of your house and your new apartment has no furniture. And, oh yeah, there are no savings. But you have a good job!) Only then would it make sense to purchase essential items with credit. And then, I would still advise to proceed with caution!

## Disappearing Assets

Let's talk about the disappearing asset. Cosmetics, food, travel come to mind immediately. It's obvious, isn't it? Do we really need to talk about this? I know, I know. You thought you could pay it off at the end of the month. Most people say they are going to do this and most people don't. It's just too easy. Next month will be better. Then there is a new "must have" or a true emergency.

Imagine a person on the edge of the Grand Canyon with a homemade flying machine. And imagine me on the sidewalk screaming, "DON'T DO IT!!" That's what I am saying about paying for disappearing assets with a credit card.

## Looking at the Big Picture

As stated above, on any and all debt, you must know the total interest you will pay over the life of the loan. Taking on a loan without having a rough idea how much your creditor is going to charge you makes no sense at all. Check this out:

- When you borrow for a car $35,000 car @ 3.5% and finance for 5 years, you will pay approximately $3,400 in interest charges.
- If you borrow for a $500,000 house with a 30-year mortgage at 3.5%, you will pay approximately $308,280 in interest over the life of the loan.
- If you have run up a $10,000 credit card bill and can only pay the minimum monthly payment of $250, at 24% you will pay *an additional* $10,318 in interest.
- If you have a $50,000 student loan with the ultra-low rate of 1.5% over 20 years, making minimum payments, you will pay more than $7,900 in interest charges.

Pause a moment to think of the money you are earning each year. Remember our first step was to acknowledge your entire income – the amount of money you have been blessed to manage. We're talking about your stewardship—how well you take care of that blessing. Now do you really want to pay $20,318 when the original value was only $10,000?

When various professionals say interest rates are so cheap, you should use credit instead of your own money, I have to scratch my head and wonder where theirs is. They are telling us that, *even if* you have the money in the bank to pay for an item, 1%, 2% or 3% is so cheap, that you should use credit instead of your own money.

That logic comes from the Keynesian Money Theorists who say it is better to use other people's money. It's better, they say, to use the bank's money to purchase your car, and use your own cash to invest and make more money. If you can take the same amount of money and make a higher return than the interest on the loan, that is the better plan, they say.

On paper, it looks good. However, if I have money saved in the bank, why would I want to spend an *extra* $7,000 for my education, an *extra* $300,000 for my home, or an *extra* $10,000 on the clothes and furniture I bought, just because the interest rate is cheap? Also, the safety test doesn't pass. What if life changes and you can't make the payments? What if something goes awry on your investment and you don't earn that higher return, but you still have the payment on the debt? The question is, do you have a Plan B for repayment?

## What is your Plan B if something goes awry?

This is what debt *really* means: I want this item. I either don't have the money to pay for this right now, or I don't want to use the money I have to pay for this item right now. I want to pay for it later or little by little.

That may be okay. But the payment amount reduces your spendable, discretionary income each month. The payment must be affordable. If you truly do pay off the credit card expenditures every month, all is well. But it only takes one upsetting month to turn everything upside down. You must (1) track how much you are adding to the card throughout the month, and (2) know your limit for being able to pay it off.

If you don't really have enough money to pay for an item, it turns into a vicious cycle that looks like this: You are spending more than you make, so you use debt to pay for it. But with this debt, comes a higher monthly bill. Now you have even less spendable income and the need to use debt again—just to get by. This is no way to live. You are digging yourself into a hole.

When you use debt, you must know that you can make the payments *and* you have an alternate plan if your income goes away.

Plan B possibilities look like this:

- If I am disabled, I have disability insurance that would cover my Essential Spending and my debt payments.
- If I lose my job, I have an Emergency Fund that will cover my Essential Spending and my Debt Payments for ___months.

- If any other catastrophe occurs, I could sell this asset for the loan value.

- I have enough equity in my home that I could use a home equity line of credit (HELOC) to pay the debt. (HELOCs are usually offered at 75% of the home's value.) I realize that I am trading one loan for another. However, the HELOC does have flexibility and perhaps a lower interest rate.

- I have cash value in my life insurance policy and I also realize that I am trading one loan for another. In this case, I am jeopardizing my life insurance policy, but getting more flexibility in the payoff. Usually this is an interest-free loan.

- As a last resort, I could take money from my 401(k) or IRA. Yes, I would be trading loans again, and there may be a penalty if I am younger than 59.5 years of age. There is no interest paid on an IRA loan, but there probably would be on the 401(k). (I understand that what I lose is growth in my retirement savings.)

Plan B can be a bit sobering. It is meant to be. Now you are seeing the *real* impact of taking on debt. There is a significant price – a cost – to be paid. Is it worth it?

## Learning About the Debt Racket

We are bombarded with credit card offers in the mailbox and plastered on every internet homepage. Every checkout clerk in a retail store will ask you if you have their store credit card. If not, "Would you like to get one and receive a 20% discount on all merchandise for today?" Every flight on commercial air-lines will include an application offer for their card. And your bank won't miss an opportunity either.

*Understand this clearly:* The credit card is a major cash cow for every vendor. It's more profitable than selling the clothes or flights or banking products. Credit card vendors love telling you that you can earn reward points or cash back. That's pennies on the dollar for them. Your use of the card is a major revenue source. You think you are getting something for free? Not a chance. Do the math. I challenge you!

Think about it. Yes, they earn money from you, the card holder, if you don't pay your balance. They add annual interest at 20% and more to your balance! That in itself is incredible. But have you thought about the fact that the retailer gives them 3-5% of every transaction? You spend $100 at a restaurant and the restaurant sends $3 to the card company. Every time you swipe the card, the card merchant receives 3%. *Every time.* It's like owning a toll booth with millions and millions of people traveling through the gate every day. Do an internet search for Mastercard® or Visa® or PayPal® as a stock investment. You will find they do very well in every economy.

With this knowledge, do you understand why your credit score is tied to your use of revolving credit? And do you understand why your bank will encourage you to have their credit cards? Do you get why we hear constantly that you must establish your credit history for good credit. (Does it really make sense if you go to a bank asking for credit, having a significant savings account and good income, to be turned down on a loan because you don't have other debts? Yet we are told that to be credit worthy, we must have some indebtedness.) Is that upside down?

The bottom line is this: **The credit scores are not for your benefit; they are for the credit card company's benefit.** It's time to look at credit in a way that is in **your best interest** instead of the credit industry's interests.

## Getting Out Of Debt

Would it make sense for you to declare a ***stop*** to spending on any new debt, like I did? Would you consider cutting up your credit cards? Most people won't. They will make every excuse, employ every possible logic before they will give up their crutch of possible overspending. If you have an emergency fund, the crutch isn't necessary.

But I understand. I, too, absolutely shuddered at not having a "safety net" of credit cards. (We'll talk more about that in the Hidden Figure #6: Assets, on a logical level.) But cutting up your credit cards, completely eliminating your opportunity to create debt, is an *emotional* hurdle, not a logical one. Dig into your feelings again about scarcity and self-sufficiency, being big enough for the task, and being in control of who you are and what you do with your money. Put on your big girl panties and deal with the fact of your income limitations, if there are any. You may not like living on that amount, but you will never be healthy financially until you spend less than you make. By using credit for your cash flow, you are creating diseased finances.

## My "Safety Rules"

- Avoid all new debt.

- Establish an Emergency Fund (sell things from your garage that you don't use, or take an extra job) that will keep you from having to borrow if your refrigerator goes out (or other such minor catastrophes come along).

- Construct a plan to pay off all debt except for your mortgage, using the Snowball Method. If your mortgage is your only debt, and you have some cash flow, do this step first, before you start paying down the mortgage. Build up your Emergency Fund to cover at least six months of Essential Spending and create a Spending Fund for your annual payments. *When that is done*, use your cash flow to make principle payments on the house.

- Use your Emergency Fund for unexpected bills and a Spending Fund to make annual payments – *not* a credit card.

# Bonus Tip

## Buying a Car

One of the biggest hurdles to getting out of debt is buying a car. Here is the worst way, the better way and the best way.

Worst: If you are trading your car every 3-5 years, taking a new loan, you are paying very little of your principal and paying mostly interest. The credit companies love you. They will take this deal all day long. That's the worst way to buy a car, unless you have money to burn.

<u>Better:</u> If your car has fallen apart and you have no savings, take a low interest loan on a car that will be stable to drive for 6-10 years. The price has to be such that you can pay it off in 3-5 years. In five years, or when it is paid off, put that same amount of money you were paying on the loan in a money market account that will earn a small amount of interest, be safe and out of your spending reach. This time you get to earn interest and not pay it. When you have enough in savings, probably another 5 years, go buy a car for cash.

<u>Best:</u> Keep your old car until there is enough money in savings to purchase another. When you have enough money to buy a carefully maintained used car, do so. You can wave cash in hand to a seller and get a better deal than you thought possible. Shop for a brand of car known to drive well and last for 10-15 years or 350,000 miles. It should be in excellent condition and with low mileage. Then take care of it. Keep it clean, and maintained with service. Now, continue putting the equivalent of a car payment back in the money market, because when there is enough money to pay cash again, you'll want to trade and re-purchase. Now you are on a roll. Not rolling in debt.

## Workbook Assignments

You will discover what you can afford when you get to Hidden Figure #5: CASH FLOW. The Success Matrix in the Workbook together are an eye opener for how debt plays into your personalized plan, and they will help you make decisions. Leave that step for later. In this step, we want to be very clear on how much debt exists, what payments are required to support the existing debt. As we discover your personal cash flow in Hidden Figure #5, we will be able to make decisions and changes for your good. For now, let's deal with *What Is*.

In your Workbook, the Worksheets on Debt will walk you through each of these steps. But I wanted to give some more detailed rationale here. It is important to understand the background issues of the debt calculations. Bear with me! We'll get through this.

Remember that your house and car payments are counted in the Essential Spending, but the principle amount of the debts are not counted. Right now, find those loan amounts— the outstanding balances on your house (residence) and/or car—if you have other loans. You will enter them into the Workbook.

Next, you need to calculate all other debts. That means your credit cards, money you owe your brother, student loans, your 401(k) and insurance policy loans—*everything*. The worksheet in your Workbook will want you to enter the principle amount of the loan, the interest rate on the loan and the monthly payment.

There are lots of tools online that can help you calculate how to pay off your debts faster. *But be careful*. If you search the internet for "debt calculator" you will find some that will tell you to consolidate your debts (these are ads for finance companies) and others that will hound you for months about a new credit card or credit score calculator. I am offering a simple tool here that will step you through your personalized plan to get out of debt. But it doesn't calculate how much interest you can save if you pay off early. Neither does it calculate a debt-free date. If you want these numbers and would rather find something online, that's fine. *Just be careful*.

If you're not sure about a required payment, here is a quick way to calculate the minimum payment on credit card debt. Multiply your balance by 4%. That will give you a monthly amount you will have to pay. Very little principle is being paid. Basically, this number allows you to tread water on your debt balance.

**Here is a Basic Loan Calculator. The Workbook calculators and more detailed.**

| Lender | Amount Owed | Interest rate | Minimum Payment |
|---|---|---|---|
| **1** | **$0.00** | **0.00%** | **$0.00** |
| 2 | $0.00 | 0.00% | $0.00 |
| 3 | $0.00 | 0.00% | $0.00 |
| 4 | $0.00 | 0.00% | $0.00 |
| 5 | $0.00 | 0.00% | $0.00 |
| 6 | $0.00 | 0.00% | $0.00 |
| | | | |
| | | | |
| | | | |
| | | | |
| Totals | $0.00 | | $0.00 |

# TAXES

*J*oanne was still in that fog after her husband's death. Then she dared to look at a piece of mail, a brokerage statement. Startled, she awoke from her fog and entered her nightmare. She wasn't completely sure how to read the statement, but one thing she could see clearly: a huge profit built up in one mutual fund. Her biggest nightmare was to go through another stock marketcrash. If it happened again, she knew this profit would evaporate in a Wall Street second. She would rather take her profits now while the price was still high rather than let the profits disappear in a market correction. She called her broker and told him to sell the shares. Twenty years of growth in a health care mutual fund had given her a 700% profit!

Here was the problem: Joanne was willing to act from chosen ignorance. She was completely unaware of basic financial facts in her life. She didn't know what her income was normally, so she didn't know what was abnormal. She didn't know she had an unusually high income for this tax year; the same year her husband had died. His business deals had brought a lot more income than normal. She didn't know what tax bracket she was in, or how that related to capital gains. She seemed to not *want* to know about tax consequences at all.

In a nutshell, Joanne acted from chosen ignorance, operating from an insistence that such subjects were too difficult for her to even consider. She didn't want to think about the definition of capital gains, much less understand its consequences. So she ignored the fact that her mutual fund profits of 700% would be taxed at a much higher rate this year, but would have been lower next year, if she had waited to sell her mutual fund shares.

Believe me, lots of people don't know basic, crucial facts about their financial lives. But those who do not know these things are in peril. Ignorance of important information has no upside. It's like you are on a hiking trail that has a 100-foot drop on one side, and you don't know about it! Joanne was on that trail. And she didn't know she was standing right next to the drop. She made her decision to take profits in a vacuum, without considering all the consequences. And worse, she didn't seek counsel from her husband's or any other competent accountant before she made the decision. Nor did she ask her broker's advice about the tax consequences of her decision.

When Joanne chose to stick her head in the sand, it meant she wanted others to *do the challenging work for her* without her even asking. Yet, because she was not informed about basic principles of taxation, she didn't know what to ask and she didn't know what information to share.

## The Big Picture

For me, taxation is about as interesting as ear wax. But choose ignorance of tax rules at your own peril; ignore tax rules and you could cause a huge problem—like the excruciating pain from an earache. I want to make sure you know the basics of our tax laws. This chapter will help you understand the principles and will help guide you. It will not help you figure your taxes or make technical decisions. You'll need a professional to do that. But knowing the basic concepts will allow you to make sense of Hidden Figure #4: Your Taxes.

First, I recommend you do an internet search for and download a current year Tax Reference Guide. Go ahead and do that now. Just enter "Tax Reference Guide" in the search bar. You'll see several come up. Just choose one for the current year. You will want to do this every year. It contains many helpful tables for your use. I'll help you decipher how to use it.

Next, find a copy of your most recent tax return. You may have saved a copy in electronic form. Or you may have a hard copy in a file drawer. If not, you should call your tax preparer and find out how to get a copy; s/he will likely be able to send it to you. If you just can't get a copy of your return, then download a blank Form 1040 from www.irs.gov. A blank copy will help you follow along. Do this now before you move on to the next section.

### The Graduated Tax

Before you can understand the numbers or intelligently analyze the data you've gathered, you'll need a basic understanding of federal income taxation. We have a graduated income tax system. If you already understand our graduated taxation and how to read your tax return, then skip to the section: **Tax Diversification.** If not, let's dig in now to understand the big picture.

Take a look at the Tax Reference guide you just downloaded. You'll see there is a box of Federal Income Tax Rate charts, probably at the top of the page. Tax Rates are in one column and a range of income is on the same row with each rising Tax Rate. As the range of income increases, so does the Tax Rate. Most people don't understand that we don't pay taxes at just one rate.

Find the Federal Income Tax chart for Single Filers. There are different scales for Married Filing Jointly, Head of Household, Single Filers and Married Filing Separately. We will look at Single Filers. Let's say you make $90,000 in taxable income; you can see the Tax Rate associated for that number is 24%. However, you can see your income tax rate for income from $0 to $9,875 is only 10%. Then, the dollars you earn from $9,875—$40,125 are taxed at 12% and your earnings from $40,125—$85,525 are taxed at 22%. Only the amount from $85,526 to $90,000 (less than $5,000) is taxed in the 24% bracket. It's true that you might say you are in the 24% tax bracket. That's where your highest earnings put you on the chart. But if you calculate the tax in each of these tax ranges, your actual tax (without any deductions, adjustments or credits) is $15,679.50. That is only 17.42% of your $90,000 earnings. That rate is called your Effective Tax Rate. (The Tax owed, divided by your Taxable Income is your Effective Tax rate.) Now do you understand the graduated tax scale? You see that there is a difference in your Highest Tax Rate and your Effective Tax Rate. Those are two numbers that go in your Success Workbook and are extremely useful as planning tools. We'll fill your numbers in the workbook when we get to the end of this chapter. For now, we need to get a few more concepts under our belts.

## Tax Diversification

Diversification is an important part of investing. You know that. How many times have you heard, "Don't put all your eggs in one basket"? That usually is applied to investing, but it is an important part of tax planning, too! There are three categories of taxation to learn about. Think about three buckets: Taxable, Tax-Deferred, and Tax-Free.

**Taxable Accounts** – All accounts are either tax-protected or taxable. Your single account, a joint account, or a revocable trust account are all taxable. They are not tax-protected (not tax-deferred) and so they are taxable. What does that mean? Whatever happens in that account is potentially taxed. Any dividends or interest paid on those accounts shows up on your Form 1099 at the end of year. You have to report those earnings as income on your Form 1040, U.S. Individual Income Tax Return. There are specific line items for such interest earnings on the form. Also, if you sell any assets from this account, that, too, creates either capital gains or capital losses. That's why we call this a taxable account.

**Tax Deferred Accounts** – On the other hand, you may also have a tax-deferred account, an account that is protected from current income taxes. This might be an IRA, an Employee Stock Ownership Plan ("ESOP") or a 401(k) plan or an annuity; anything that doesn't send 1099 forms every year. Whatever happens in this account, stays in this account. Dividends can be paid, interest can be credited, and you can sell stock at a gain or a loss—and nothing is reported to the IRS that year. You have no tax consequences *as long as* the money stays inside the account.

**Tax Free Assets** – There are also accounts and investments that don't create taxes now or later. That may surprise you. But it is likely that you have heard or know about at least one of these types of accounts. Tax-free municipal bonds are widely known investments. They are not for everyone. They are only appropriate for those in high tax brackets (33% or higher) and they are only appropriately held in a taxable account.

Here is the rationale: Tax-free bonds pay a lower interest rate. You do report this interest income on your Form 1040, but the tax calculated on that income is zero. No taxes due! But if your tax rate is less than 33%, your tax-free return is not likely an advantage. You could have invested in taxable bonds (paying a higher interest rate), paid your taxes and still have had a higher net return than you would have in tax-free bonds. The deciding factor is your tax rate.

And why should you only own tax-free bonds in a taxable account? Because dividends and interest earned in a tax-deferred account are not taxable anyway! So accepting the lower interest rate normally paid on municipals bonds wouldn't make sense. If you have a broker or financial advisor who is recommending purchasing tax-free mutual funds or tax-free bonds inside an IRA or an annuity... get another broker. However, if you are in a tax bracket of 33% or higher, and you need to buy bonds in a taxable account in order to balance your portfolio, looking for tax-free municipal bonds is a reasonable choice.

Permanent life insurance can also work well as a tax-free vehicle for accumulation. As always, there are pros and cons for the strategy. You must buy the policy at the right time in your life, before life insurance gets too expensive and you must buy from a company that is set up for this type of accumulation plan. The laws regarding life insurance were established in the early years of our IRS code. If you read IRS code 79, you'll see that tremendous advantage is given to those who want to accumulate wealth in a permanent life policy. Everything grows tax-deferred like retirement accounts, but eventually, in a tax-deferred account, you will be required to take the money out and pay taxes on it (RMDs – Required Minimum Distributions – are the designation given to these mandatory withdrawals that subject those withdrawals to income taxation). Not so with life insurance cash value. When you take money out, you "borrow" your own money (usually interest-free) without any taxes due.

Many people find this hard to believe, and determine that it must be some kind of fraud or trick from the insurance company. I assure you that it is legitimate, legal, and worthy of consideration. You must have a legitimate need for life insurance, be relatively healthy, be able to afford and willing to pay the higher insurance premiums of a whole life policy. But if these requirements are met, the accumulation is real, is not at risk in the stock market and you can access the growth without being taxed. I recommend that you talk to a reputable, large life insurance company like Mass Mutual, Nationwide,

Prudential, or Allianz. They all have excellent products in this area. You can do an internet search for "tax-free accumulations in an insurance policy."

Roth IRAs and Roth 401(k)s are better-known tax-free strategies. They are after-tax contributions that **accumulate earnings tax-free** and the distributions are tax-free. Eligibility is based on your income level, which is defined as your Modified Adjusted Gross Income (MAGI). You are eligible for a $6,000 per year contribution, or $7,000 if over age 50, *if* you make less than the Phase-Out MAGI, as noted in the 2020 Tax Reference Guide.

If you check out your 2020 Tax Reference Guide, you will see that a Roth IRA contribution is not available if you make more than $139,000 as a Single Filer or $206,000 as a Married Filer. *However*, if your employer offers a Roth 401(k) contribution choice, you don't have to worry about the Phase-Out rule. In neither of these accounts will you get to make a deduction for a Roth contribution. The advantage is that you will not have to pay any taxes when you take money out of that Roth IRA, as long as your contribution was held at least 5 years in the Roth account. All tax-free. And that's nice. If you have enough deductions *and* you believe that taxes will likely be higher when you retire, this may be an excellent strategy for you.

Many people arrive a few years away from retirement with two buckets: taxable and tax-deferred. They have totally forgotten the third bucket: tax-free. If the IRA is large, they are seeing that perhaps their largest bill in retirement will be the tax bill. "Oh no!" they say. "Can I do a Roth?"

That is rarely a workable plan, since it would cause a big taxable event if they take money out of the IRA to contribute to the Roth. It can be done, but is it an advantage? Speak to your tax professional before proceeding!

It also takes planning from an earlier age to make the insurance accumulations work. If you have waited for this tax-diversification planning, municipal bonds are usually your only option for a tax-free strategy.

Choosing a strategy for owning all three buckets is an important conversation to have with your broker or financial advisor or tax advisor, years before retirement. Hopefully, you are now empowered to address the concerns and have a meaningful conversation!

## Tax Efficiency

There are some important nuances in getting your money more tax efficient while it is growing. Being tax efficient means you are paying less in taxes. First let's discuss how timing some required liquidations can be made more tax efficient as well as cost efficient. Then let's talk about which assets/investments should be located in which accounts, in order to reduce taxes.

### Capital Gains Taxes

Different types of income, like Social Security and investment income, have their own calculations and tax schedules. One frequently confused income is from Capital Gains. Just knowing a little bit about this would have saved Joanne a boatload in taxes. Capital Gains Tax is a tax assessed when you are selling an asset for a profit. The asset may be a business, a stock, a real estate parcel, or any other item you own. If you own an asset and sell it for a profit, you will be reporting Capital Gains. (If you sell it for a loss, you will report a Capital Loss, which will be subtracted from your Capital Gains.) Before you get infatuated with taking a profit and seeing dollar signs in your dreams, stop and consider the tax ramifications. There may be a better way or time to take those profits. A good tax advisor is worth a lot. Just stop, consider, and get some advice.

Here is a basic explanation. The Capital Gains tax is a lower and different rate than your income tax. The higher your income tax rate, the higher your Capital Gains rate is. Your Capital Gains rate will be a graduated scale of 0%, 15%, or 20%, corresponding to each of your income tax rates. I strongly recommend that you let a tax professional help you with this. But just knowing that it is possible to pay 0% Capital Gains Tax if you have earned less than $40,125 as a Single Tax Filer or $80,250 as a Joint Filer should make you sit up and take note. In other words, if you have a low-income year, it may be a good time to sell real estate, restricted stock, or any investment in a profitable situation. Many people retire with a large amount of company stock. If you are careful, and choose low income years in which to sell it, you could potentially pay very little in Capital Gains Tax. The opposite is true as well. If this is a high income year for you, you must think carefully about selling an asset. Careful planning is a must for you.

Any year when earnings fluctuate, you have an opportunity to do some tax planning. Seek out advice to take advantage before the year ends. Note: taxes may be due in April of the next year, but all transactions must be completed by December 31 of the tax year.

## Unearned Income

**Take special note** if you are retired or live off of investment income. Tax costs can jump considerably if your **Unearned Income** increases over certain thresholds. Look in the Tax Reference Guide for the Medicare Contribution Tax. (And there is no table for Alternative Minimum Tax, because of its complexity. You will need a tax professional to figure this one, for sure!) If you have a large investment portfolio, and you are near the edge of the bracket for one of these additional taxes, you should talk to your tax advisor or your broker about strategies. Again, I am not here to instruct you on tax calculations. I simply want to make you aware of how the system works.

## IRA Contributions and Distributions

As long as you have *earned* income, you can make IRA contributions. These contributions have limits, and you should check the Tax Reference Guide to see how much you can contribute. If you are over age 50, you can contribute more than those under age 50. Depending on how much money you make, your contribution may or may not be deductible. These limits vary and are shown in the tax reference tables.

Taking money out of an IRA or tax-deferred account is pretty straightforward. Taking money out is called a distribution. If your contribution was tax-deductible, you will have to pay income taxes when you take a distribution. Study the Form 1040 which you downloaded or your own 1040 from last year's tax filing. You will see the line where you report IRA distributions. Your taxes will be calculated at whatever rate is correct for your total income. Remember, you got the benefit of deducting your contributions from your gross income at the time you made those contributions. You never paid taxes on that money. And as the account grew, you got to defer the tax on the growth. It's like that money was behind a firewall from the IRS. So when you take money out from behind that firewall, you must report that distribution income to the IRS for tax purposes. Every dollar of distributions is taxable at Income Tax rates, not Capital Gains rates.

You may want to re-read the section above on tax diversification. It is not always advisable to make your tax-deferred retirement account the only place you are accumulating for retirement. Sometimes the biggest bill retirees pay is their tax bill. Pre-retirement planning is needed to avoid this.

By the way, if you are taking a distribution from a tax-deferred account before age 59½, you will be assessed a penalty of 10% in addition to your income taxes due. There are, of course, some exceptions for the rule. Please check with your tax advisor before you take money out. Your IRA should be your last resort for accessing money.

## Required Minimum Distributions

The IRS has a liquidation plan for your IRA. As mentioned earlier, the liquidation plan is called "Required Minimum Distributions (RMDs)" Currently, when you reach age 72 you are required to take money out of the IRA. You *must* take this distribution whether you want or need income. The IRS has been patiently waiting and it now dictates the amount you must liquidate. Look on the Tax Reference Guide, page 2, Uniform Lifetime Table. The total of your IRA accounts must be divided by the Divisor Balance for your age. For example, if you have $100,000 in an IRA and you are 75 years old, you will need to divide your balance by 22.9. That equals $4,366.81. You will need to withdraw that amount from your IRA by December 31 and report that income for the current taxable year. If you are 76, you divide your balance by 22. Every year, the divisor gets smaller, because it is assumed your life expectancy just got shorter.

It doesn't matter if you put the money in your checking account and spend it, give it away, or put it in a taxable account to be reinvested. But you **must** take the Required Minimum Distribution each year, calculated by the formula given in the Tax Reference Guide.

Some people prefer to set up an automatic liquidation every month, so that assets will have a dollar cost averaging effect. Others prefer to liquidate once per year, to make sure it gets done. Doing it right is important! The IRS assesses a 50% penalty on missing your RMD!

To minimize your taxes, commissions, and loss of profits, consider the following strategies when you take your RMDs. If you rebalance your portfolio on a regular basis, (and you should) and find you are selling one asset class to keep your asset mix (*i.e.*, 60% stocks/ 40% bonds) then you might move the "sells" out of the IRA to count toward your RMDs that year, rather than reinvesting the proceeds of your sale, only to have to sell again later for RMD distributions. Doing the rebalance and taking RMDs all at the same time makes sense. Your broker should do this for you. Consider this strategy during your tax evaluation time and discuss it with your broker. Planning can also help you avoid selling in a down market.

Keep in mind that mutual funds generally have a big pay-out of Capital Gains distributions at the end of the year. If you own mutual funds in your IRA, you can have these pay-outs as a part of your RMD also, rather than have another selling event to create the cash. Dividends also can be paying out all year, counting toward your RMD, rather than having to sell shares of your mutual funds.

## Location Tax Efficiency

Locating the right assets in the right types of accounts is another way to save on taxes. Generally speaking, keep your securities that produce the most income in your IRA, where they are tax protected. Those securities would be taxable bonds, income mutual funds, high yield funds, stocks paying high dividends ("Income Mutual Funds) or stock funds that have a high Capital Gains distribution (these are funds that have a high turnover rate).

Locate assets with buy and hold strategies of growth stock in your taxable accounts. Very little taxes will be created by these types of securities because they produce low dividends (below 2%) and therefore create Capital Gains taxes only when you infrequently sell to take profits.

## Accept The Good With The Bad

Nothing is sure but death and taxes, so the saying goes. Taxation is a part of being *blessed* with income sources. Awareness can help you keep more of your money in your own pocket, and help you make better choices. I would never advise someone to leave money on the table to avoid paying more taxes. In other words, don't turn down income or the opportunity to make money because taxes would be due. Paying taxes is simply a part of the money-making process. Plenty of bad decisions have been made on the basis of avoiding taxes. Let's avoid this. Let's just be prepared and efficient.

## Ways to Reduce Taxable Income

If you want to reduce your taxable income for the year, there are a couple of ways to help yourself realize that objective.

One, give some money to a charity. That's always a gratifying and smart thing to do! I love giving to my favorite charities. Whatever your cause – education, feeding the poor, housing the homeless, giving medical help to those in need – do it! Our nation was founded on the belief that those who have more should and will help those with less. Our government approves! Tax laws are based on giving citizens an incentive to do certain things. Our tax laws make it advantageous for us to give, and charities to receive! I love that.

Second, contribute to your retirement account. Remember one way to reduce your current-year income taxes is by contributing to a qualified retirement account. If you are an employee, you can reduce your taxable income by as much as $19,000, or if you are over age 50, $25,500, by contributing to your 401(k). If you are self-employed, you should have a SEP (Simplified Employee Pension Plan) or individual 401(k) or one of the other types of Qualified Plans. The maximum contributions vary with each plan, but all may offer you a big advantage in reducing your taxable income. I recommend a conversation with a small business specialist who knows tax law. Almost every financial broker-dealer will have specialists on hand. Ask your broker to refer you. These deductions are enough to drop you down to a lower tax bracket in some cases. That's really significant. Know your maximum contribution and take advantage.

Investments in income property real estate can also be a great way to reduce your income taxes. Rental property generally allows significant itemized deductions. For all the work and heartache that sometimes goes along with rentals, it may offer you great relief from taxes.

Any legally organized home business can produce tax deductions. I recommend you read RICH DAD POOR DAD[4] for more understanding in this area. Some great concepts are taught here!

## Avoiding Mistakes

Mistakes happen, but if the IRS suspects you made more than a mistake — you actually were trying to defraud — you could end up with a full-blown audit and penalties.

Here are a few key tax mistakes that you should be very careful to avoid:

One is inflating your expenses for business. Claim only the expenses you can document. And your deductions should be ordinary and necessary costs for doing business. Don't fudge the lines between office and personal expenses.

Here's a similar word about charities. You can't gather your worn-out junk, give it to Goodwill, and claim you gave away designer items from your closet. You need pictures and receipts of what you donated. And for heaven's sake, make sure your donation was to a legitimate 501(c)(3) charity. Stick to name brand charities. Sometimes, fraudsters will alter the name just

[4] R. Kiyosaki and S. Lechter, RICH DAD, POOR DAD, Warner Books Ed, New York, NY (1997).

slightly from recognizable organizations. Don't make quick decisions to donate to something you just saw on TV. Know who the intended recipient of your gift is. Check them out on the IRS website, IRS.gov. In your browser "search" bar, type "exempt organizations." You will find lists upon lists. Your group should be on that list or your "donation" may get you in trouble.

If you give *more* than $15,000 as an individual or $30,000 as a married couple, your will need to report it on your tax return. The amount over your limit is deducted from your life-time gift tax exemption. Talk to your tax advisor to avoid a possibly-crucial mistake that may increase gift and estate taxes in the settlement of your estate.

## Your Personal Tax Planning Meeting

Remember that the purpose of learning a bit about our tax code is to help you save money. I hope this wasn't too tedious for you! No matter how uninteresting the subject of taxation is, saving money is interesting ... right? In fact, I recommend taking a pause every year to consider where you are in your annual earnings and where you might save in taxes. In your Success Workbook, in the last chapter, "Pulling it all Together", you will be given a list of questions and analysis sequence for an annual meeting with your tax expert. Just understanding these principles is extremely helpful when you get to that Personal Tax Planning Meeting (PTPM).

### Reflecting

You have accomplished a lot at this point! Step back for a moment and think of it! You have calculated, analyzed and recorded the first four of your personal Hidden Figures: Income, Spending, Debts, and Taxes. You know how much work and knowledge – awareness - goes into knowing and understanding your own personal Hidden Figures. You know how much money you need to survive and how much money it takes to support your lifestyle. You have considered your options and desires concerning debt. Hopefully, you came up with some ideas about what is really important to you and are formulating some ideas on how to improve things. Now, in this chapter, we have explored ways to plan for your taxes. Please take some time to appreciate how far you have come! You deserve it!

## SUPPLEMENTAL INFORMATION
## FOR YOUR WORKBOOK

This chapter is a project in discovery. You are going to get a clearer picture of your taxes than you thought possible! Because this information is so lengthy, it is listed here instead of in the Workbook. As you discover each number, turn to your Workbook in the Taxes Worksheet section. Find "Important Tax Numbers" and one by one, document your discoveries.

- Open your latest tax return filing document. Or choose a blank copy of Form 1040. (If you have a copy of 2018 or earlier Forms 1040, you will see that the locations of some line items have changed. But it is all there. Just look for the terms listed in bold.

- We will be discussing the following: **Total Income, line 7b; Adjusted Gross Income, line 8a; Deductions, lines 9 and 10; Taxable Income, line 11b; Tax, line 12a and Total Tax, line 16**. Please highlight these lines on your tax Form 1040. All of these numbers will be transferred to your Success Workbook.

- Let's start with **Total Income.** Find it on line 7b. That is a total of your wages, plus any tax-exempt interest, IRA distributions, dividends, Social Security, *etc*. Some of those types of income must be run through a different calculation or grid to see if they are really taxable and if so, at what rate. But your **Total Income** is going to include it all. Add this number to your Personalized Tax Chart below.

- **Adjusted Gross Income** is your "Gross" income before you pay taxes but after you have "Adjusted" it for certain types of income or excluded income. You may or may not have some of those adjustments applied to your income. You can compare line 7b to line 8b to see if there is any difference. Make a note of your **Adjusted Gross Income (AGI)** on line 8b. Add it to your chart below.

- Now notice lines 9 and 10 on the 1040 form. These are **Deductions.** You can see that you either subtracted the standard deduction or you used itemized deductions. Also, see if you subtracted qualified business expenses.

- Note line 11b, your **Taxable Income**. That is your **Adjusted Gross Income** minus your **Deductions**. Notice your **Taxable Income** and how it differs from your **Total Income**. Enter your **Taxable Income** on the chart.

- Once the **Tax** is figured on the graduated scale, that calculation is entered on line 12a. Enter your **Tax** from 12a on the chart.

- Lines 13a to 15 are commonly referred to as "below the line" deductions and are the most valuable deductions. They are called "credits" and are dollar-for-dollar savings in the taxes owed and they include everything from self-employment taxes to other taxes paid to child tax credits. If any numbers exist on lines 13-15 in your tax form, total them and write them on your chart as **Tax Credits.**

- Find **Total Tax** on line 16. It is the calculation of tax owed after those important credits are subtracted. This is what must be paid to the Internal Revenue Service this year. You get to subtract the amount of taxes you have already paid in (*i.e.*, quarterly tax estimates paid or taxes withheld from your wages, or taxes on account withdrawals and distributions, plus taxes deducted on Social Security benefits). Whatever you haven't already paid, you must now pay. If you paid in too much, you will claim a refund. Please enter your **Total Tax** on your chart.

You can see that your last year's tax return has a lot of information for you! You've probably never thought of it as good reading material. But I do encourage you to read it through one time each year and refresh your knowledge of income taxation and how it affects you. Every term mentioned here is important information and affects your financial health.

- Your next assignment is to look at the Tax Reference Chart and find your highest tax rate. That is found by taking your **Total Income** and finding the tax rate associated with that earning level. Write that number on your chart.
- Take the **Total Tax** owed and divide it by your **Total Income**. That is your **Effective Tax Rate**.
- The chart below is duplicated in your Workbook.

## Important Tax Numbers

| Important Tax Numbers | | | |
|---|---|---|---|
| Total Income | | Top Tax Rate | |
| Adjusted Gross Income (AGI ) | | | |
| Deductions | | | |
| Taxable Income | | | |
| Tax | | | |
| Tax Credits | | | |
| Total Tax | | Effective Tax Rate | |
| | | | |

You have now completed Income and Expenses. Great accomplishment! Now let's move on to talk about **Cash Flow. This is where is get's *really* interesting!**

# CASH FLOW

*M*ary had made great progress since I last saw her. She had successfully landed a position with an estate planning firm where she received an average gross income of $175,000 and her net income (after taxes) was $136,500. Mary was settling into her new life after the divorce and I was happy to see her doing so well. She knew our next step was working on her spending. "But first," she said, "can you help me allocate my new 401(k) and invest a small inheritance from my grandmother?"

"Sure," I said. "How much are you saving for retirement now, Mary?"

"Not any, right now."

"Why is that? "

"I can't afford it. I get to the end of every month completely out of money."

"Well, it's impossible to save for retirement then, isn't it? Let's get to the root of this. Can we go back to the original plan and talk about your spending?"

**It's so easy to get ahead of ourselves.** We want to talk about saving for retirement when the real issue at hand is how much we are spending on doodads. Mary estimated she was spending approximately $8,000 per month. We multiplied that by 12 and rounded up to get an annualized sum of $100,000 for expenses. I wanted her estimate first before we looked at the actual numbers. And, like most people, she was shocked by the real numbers.

We printed an "account activity" for the last 90 days on her bank and credit card accounts. Every expenditure went into one of four columns: (1) Essential Spending (2) Non-Essential, Lifestyle Spending (3) Federal Income Taxes, and (4) Debt Payments. (Remember the Essential and Non-Essential Spending are defined in Hidden Figure #2. Review the chapter if needed.) We needed annualized totals so we took the total from each column (90 days) and then multiplied by four.

The point of totaling expenses is to calculate Cash Flow. Cash Flow is a simple arithmetic problem. Take your Total Income and subtract your Total Expenses. The difference is your Cash Flow. We hope to see a positive number here. In other words, we want to see that there is money left over after your expenses. Why? SO YOU CAN SAVE SOME MONEY. If your Cash Flow is positive, and you save or invest that money, your financial security will increase. The opposite is also true. If Cash Flow is negative, your financial security will decrease. You must do whatever it takes to make your Cash Flow a positive number. You've heard this before, but I'll say it again.

**You will never be financially healthy unless you spend less than you make.**

## Accumulation Phase or Distribution Phase?

Are you still working and building up savings so that you can someday live on your savings? If so, you are in the Accumulation Phase.

Or, are you no longer working and using your savings to supply or supplement your income? If so, you are in the Distribution Phase. That's what retirement is. In retirement, you are no longer actively accumulating wealth. You are distributing your wealth. If you are retired, it is expected that your expenses are outstripping your income. You have built up your savings to a point so that you can afford to liquidate a portion of your savings each year. You have planned for this liquidation. Ideally, I recommend you use your guaranteed income (Social Security, Pensions, and Annuities) to fund your Essential Spending. Your Non-Essential Spending can be deducted from your other savings and investment assets. That's my idea of a secure retirement. Please work with your financial planner to determine how much you can safely liquidate each year so that you don't run out of money. It's nice to know that whatever the stock market does, your Essential Spending is being covered by a guaranteed check every month. You can pull back or splurge with the Non-Essential Spending, based on the market moves.

However, if you are in the Accumulation Phase of your financial life, you must ensure your expenses are smaller than your income. This truth is graphically shown on the Success

Matrix. If your Cash Flow is negative (shown with parentheses around it), you are spending more than you earn. Your financial security will diminish. If your Cash Flow is negative you are spending money you don't have. Usually, you are adding to your credit card debt.

There is another possibility. You could be spending from your assets. If you are an accumulator, this is still negative Cash Flow. If you have cash in your checking account, savings account, or a brokerage account, you could be spending those assets to pay for your excess. We'll talk about Net Worth in Hidden Figures #7. For now, just know that spending your assets lowers your Net Worth year over year. That's not a good trajectory.

For instance, you may be earning $75,000 but spending $100,000. If you are liquidating $25,000 of your brokerage account to cover the excess spending, you will decrease your Net Worth.

When Mary saw her success Matrix, this was her moment of bare-knuckle truth.

## Exhibit 1: Mary's Current Success Matrix

| Gross Income | | Expenses | | Cash Flow |
|---|---|---|---|---|
| Total Guaranteed Income | 0 | Essential spending | $75,000 | |
| Total Other Income | $175,000 | Non-Essential Lifestyle | 60,000 | |
| | | Debt Pmts | | |
| | | Credit Card | 16,800 | |
| | | Income Taxes | 39,072 | |
| **Total Income** | **$175,000** | | **$190,872** | **Cash Flow** $(15,872) |
| **Assets** | | **Liabilities** | | **Net Worth** |
| Cash | $5,000 | Credit Cards | $35,000 | |
| Emergency Savings | 0 | | | |
| Savings | 55,000 | | | |
| Financial Investments | 0 | | | |
| Home | 1,290,000 | Mortgage | 1,100,000 | |
| Car | 15,000 | Car | 30,000 | |
| | 0 | | | |
| **Total Assets** | **$1,365,000** | | **$1,165,000** | **Net Worth** $200,000 |

Here was Mary's reality. She was spending $190,872 not $100,000 as she estimated. By following the chart below, you see the Cash Flow is ($15,872), a negative number. In other words, she was spending $15,872 per year that she didn't have. Her credit card company was loaning her this money. And she was paying them 24% annually for this privilege. My calculations showed an estimate of next year's debt (in the liability section) increasing to $50,872. By next year, her debt payments will have increased to $2,034 a month, or $24,418 annually. Her Cash Flow would be even more negative. And her Net Worth will drop significantly. You can see clearly that this is not a sustainable plan.

A decreasing Net Worth year by year guarantees you will run out of money, be unable to pay your bills, and never retire. What do you imagine this would look like in two or three more years? Do you see why Mary needed to change some habits?

# Exhibit 2: Mary's Success Matrix in 1 yr with No Spending Changes

| Gross Income | | Expenses | | Cash Flow |
|---|---|---|---|---|
| Total Guaranteed Income | 0 | Essential spending | $75,000 | |
| Total Other Income | $175,000 | Non-Essential Lifestyle | 60,000 | |
| | | Debt Payments | | |
| | | Credit Card | 24,418 | |
| | | Income Taxes | 39,072 | |
| Total Income | $175,000 | | $198,490 | Cash Flow ($23,490) |

| Assets | | Liabilities | | Net Worth |
|---|---|---|---|---|
| Cash in checking Acct | $5,000 | Credit Cards | $50,872 | |
| Emergency Savings | 0 | | | |
| Savings | 55,000 | | | |
| Financial Investments | | | | |
| Home | 1,290,000 | Mortgage | 1,100,000 | |
| Car | 15,000 | Car | 30,000 | |
| Total Assets | $1,365,000 | | $1,180,872 | Net Worth $184,128 |

Looking again at her current Success Matrix, we acknowledged that she could do nothing about her federal income taxes, unless she contributed to her 401(k). But until she had her Cash Flow under control, I didn't recommend adding to her assets while her liabilities were continuing to increase. Every expense had to be examined. Line by line, we needed to consider what was best to do.

Every month, Mary was spending almost $5,000 on clothes, concert tickets, weekend getaways, and restaurants. Admittedly, a lot of this was an expectation of her teenage girls. Wide eyed, Mary saw that a frank family discussion was in order. The $15,872 of negative Cash Flow was reflective of entitlement thinking by all of them. She knew this had to be changed – and fast!

Remember, Cash Flow is just an arithmetic problem. Total income – Total Expenses. So, there is a subtler question that arises in this analysis:

"Mary, do you remember that your estimate of spending was around $100,000? Why do you think you are spending an additional $91,000 without knowing it?" I asked.

"Well, since the divorce, I honestly haven't looked at my spending. "I could see Mary shift in her chair … and shift in her thinking. "I have been angry and wanted to feel good about myself. When I was married and we had two incomes, we had money to spend like that. I haven't wanted to face up to what the divorce means to me in terms of changes in spending habits. It's scary!"

"Of course," I sympathized. "It's a huge adjustment."

"I knew something was off," she continued. "I used to have money to do whatever I wanted. When I got my new job, I signed up for the 401(k) as soon as I could. Then I just couldn't make ends meet. I had to quit. And I have this niggling fear that I'll be poor and destitute when I'm old and ready to retire."

"Now that we've done this little exercise, what do you see as the solution?" I asked.

"I need to spend less, for sure."

"Any idea where to start on that?"

"No more credit card expenditures!"

"Good! Can you be more specific? If you stop spending right now and tear up the credit cards, you still have the existing debt. You owe $35,000 to the credit card companies, right? Each month, you will not only have to *not* add to the balance, you will need to lower the balance. So that increases your spending temporarily. Our minimum goal is to get the Total Expenses to equal the Total Income. But *your* stated goal is to save for retirement. To do that, Expenses should be *lower* than your Income so that you have a surplus, a positive Cash Flow. Any idea what we could do to lower your Expenses?

"I could just quit buying any concert tickets and clothes. Really tighten my belt."

"Yes, you could," I encouraged. "This should be an opportunity for you to look closely at what is important to you as a measure of quality of life. In other words, where do you spend rather carelessly and needlessly, and what is meaningful? Most people have a minimum of $1,500 a month that they have no idea about where it is being spent, and the expenditures actually mean very little to them. I'd bet a latte that is true for you."

"Yeah. I obviously have more like $5,000 per month that I wasn't aware I was spending!"

"Let's look at each line of your expenses. Starting with Essential Spending, is there anything there that could be reduced?"

That brought up a whole new discussion about the big house she was living in. She was awarded the house, along with the mortgage, as part of her settlement in the divorce decree. She admitted that it was more house than she wanted or needed now. It was no longer her dream to live in a ritzy neighborhood. She needed to re-evaluate this expense. Although the mortgage was a low interest rate, her payment was still more than $4,000 a month. She could probably sell the house at a profit and get a smaller house; smaller payment, and significantly reduce her Essential Spending. After some research and more discussion, Mary came up with the following ideas:

a. Sell the house. After paying off the mortgage, and realtor she could set aside enough money for a down payment on a smaller home and still have $15,000 left to pay off some debt.

b. Buying a smaller home closer to the girl's schools would have an advantage of saving some time, give her a smaller yard to care for, and smaller $2,800/month mortgage. That would reduce her Essential Spending by $14,400, down to a more manageable amount of $60,600 annually.

c. Reduce the Non-Essential Lifestyle spending to $3,500 per month, making it $42,000 annually.

d. Then apply the $15,000 profit on the sale of the large house to pay down on the credit card, along with her decisions to -

    a. Commit to no new expenses on the card, and

    b. By increasing her payment on the credit card just slightly, actually start paying down principal.

## Exhibit 3: Mary Reduces Spending; Buys a Smaller Home

| Gross Income | | Expenses | | Cash Flow |
|---|---|---|---|---|
| Total Guaranteed Income | 0 | Essential spending | $60,600 | |
| Total Other Income | $175,000 | Non-Essential Lifestyle | 42,000 | |
| | - | Debt Pmts | | |
| | | Credit Card | 9,600 | |
| | | Income Taxes | 38,500 | |
| **Total Income** | **$175,000** | | **$150,700** | **Cash Flow** | **$24,300** |

| Assets | | Liabilities | | Net Worth |
|---|---|---|---|---|
| Cash in checking Acct | $5,000 | Credit Cards | 20,000 | |
| Emergency Savings | 0 | | | |
| Savings | 55,000 | | | |
| Financial Investments | 16,500 | | | |
| Home | 700,000 | Mortgage | 690,000 | |
| Car | 15,000 | Car | 29,000 | |
| **Total Assets** | **$791,500** | | **$739,000** | **Net Worth** | **$52,500** |

Note the differences:

- What happened to Mary's Cash Flow when these adjustments were made? She was finally in a positive cash flow! She now had almost $16,500 she could add to her 401(k).

- We are keeping this simple here, but in reality, when Mary contributed to her 401(k), she reduced her taxable income. That, in turn, reduces her federal income taxes. And that, in turn, also increases her cash flow. We will not try to illustrate this here, but note that this has a *Spiraling Good Effect*.

- The result of investing in the 401(k) would be that by next year, Mary's assets would have another line item in the total, showing $16,500 in financial assets.

- Do you see the difference in her Net Worth? It is less! What happened?

  o She sold her expensive house. Her new home had lower market value and because she was starting over on the mortgage, she now has very little equity. So that hurt her Net Worth for now. Think of how this will change in the future. Because the house is an appreciating asset, her Net Worth will increase in years to come: The value of the home will go up. At the same time, the mortgage, as a Liability, will go down. As long as she has income to pay the mortgage, this is also a *Spiraling Good Effect*.

  o What is the effect of taking $15,000 from the net profit (after repairs, realtor fees, and new down payment) from the house sale and paying down her debt? Do you see she has lower Liabilities—less debt—to subtract from her Assets? Do you also see that her credit card payments have decreased? Aha! another *Spiraling Good Effect!*

○ Compare her Net Worth in Exhibit 3 with Exhibit 2 (leaving spending as is). Even though her Net Worth is much lower, she also has less debt and more appreciating assets. With all those *Spiraling Good Effects*, her future is going to be brighter.

● Mary's main advantage from this Plan B is that she has created a positive Cash Flow and can see an upward trajectory in her financial Net Worth.

● Do you also see that there is more safety in Mary's financial situation? Mary's initial instincts were telling her she was not in a safe place with her financial picture. In Mary's Success Matrix 3, we have increased Cash Flow and decreased Debt. These are always steps to greater safety.

# Spiraling Good Effects

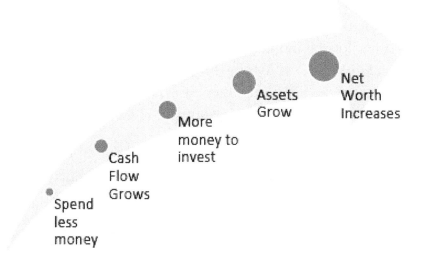

# Spiraling Bad Effects

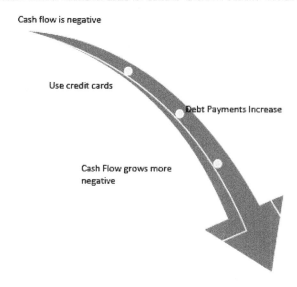

Mary was so encouraged about this possibility, she decided to look at her inheritance funds of $55,000 and consider paying debt down even further. She had originally thought this investment could go toward some aggressive mutual fund and earn her lots of money. When she caught on to the concept of building her Net Worth through positive Cash Flow and eliminating the debt drag, there was no stopping Mary! This was way better than a risky investment! Here are the next steps she took:

- She took three steps with her $55,000 inheritance money.
  - She set up $30,000 in an emergency fund in a higher paying money market fund.
  - She used $20,000 to pay off the rest of her credit card debt.
  - That left $5,000 to reduce her remaining debt—her car. That move allowed her to pay off the car one year earlier than scheduled and in the long run she saved a couple of thousand dollars in finance charges!

Note the changes in her Matrix now.

# Exhibit 4: Mary Pays Down Debt and Increases Savings

| Gross Income | | Expenses | | Cash Flow |
|---|---|---|---|---|
| Total Guaranteed Income | 0 | Essential spending | $60,600 | |
| Total Other Income | $175,000 | Non-Essential Lifestyle | 42,000 | |
| | - | Debt Payments | 0 | |
| | | Credit Card | 0 | |
| | | Car | 7,800 | |
| | | Federal & State Income Taxes | 38,500 | |
| Total Income | $175,000 | Total Income | $148,900 | Cash Flow | $26,100 |

| Assets | | Liabilities | | Net Worth |
|---|---|---|---|---|
| Cash in checking Acct | $5,000 | Credit Cards | 0 | |
| Emergency Savings | 30,000 | | | |
| Savings | 0 | | | |
| Financial Investments | 42,600 | | | |
| Home | 700,000 | Mortgage | 688,000 | |
| Car | 12,000 | Car | 22,000 | |
| Total Assets | $789,600 | | $710,000 | Net Worth | $79,600 |

Note the following items:

- What is her new Cash Flow? She now has enough Cash Flow to max out her 401(k) contributions and possibly add some to a brokerage account. (Maybe buying the aggressive mutual fund she wanted in the first place?)
- Check out the assets now. She has $42,600 in Financial Assets (401(k) + brokerage account)
- The Savings account has been zeroed out. Instead she now has $30,000 in Emergency Funds, ensuring she will be able to meet an unforeseen event without using the credit card.
- Note the car value and the car loan value. The car is a depreciating asset, so it went down. But her loan went down more (since she paid $5,000 from the savings account).
- In total, Mary's Net Worth went up $27,100!
- As noted before, she increased her financial safety level by establishing an emergency fund, decreasing her debt further and increasing her savings.

## Creating Your Best Spending Plan

By seeing Mary's progression and improved financial position, perhaps you can envision your own new path to financial security. Each path is unique and has to be tackled with a creative, determined mindset.

When Barbara came to me, she was trapped in scarcity thinking. Her husband was now totally dependent on her, thinking much like a child about what they would do each day. She had to keep her massive fears stuffed inside so as not to upset him. How much money would it take for his medical care? Would they be able to find a new house they could afford? Would they run out of money? As Barbara started on this task of filling out her Success Matrix, she was frightened... the future was so uncertain. But not understanding the purpose of each asset class was an even bigger source of her fear. Creating Barbara's path to success required a completely different set of solutions than Mary's. You'll see her progression in Hidden Figure #6: Assets, just ahead.

## Workbook Assignments

Cash flow assignments await you in the Workbook! Purchase the workbook here: www.MyHiddenFigures.net.

# ASSETS

*A*ssets are things you own, things that are marketable and have a potential for growing in value. Certain categories of assets have similar attributes, like *volatility* (how much the price fluctuates), *liquidity* (how easily you can sell an item and convert to cash), and *appreciation rates* (the average rate an item grows in value). There is no perfect asset. There is nothing that has only positive attributes and no negatives. Every group or type of asset grows in value and has a potential gain and a potential loss – an upside and a downside. Anytime you are considering putting money in or adding money to an asset, you should be clear, very clear on what these attributes are.

In general, assets have a trade-off in growth and liquidity, risk and reward. The more liquid an asset is, the less likely it is to grow or outpace inflation. Liquid assets have low risk, but also relatively low reward. If the asset is harder to sell or takes longer to grow, then it likely has a tendency toward higher reward. Growth assets have a higher risk and also a higher reward.

Generally, assets are grouped into four categories: (1) Cash; (2) Financial Investments; (3) Real Estate; (4) Hard Assets.

## Barbara vs. Cash

"Hello?" Barbara answered as she tried to catch her breath. She had run from her husband's day bed to find her phone. She had spent most of the day coaxing him to get dressed ... it was one of those days. Everything was an uphill battle.

Barbara had taken the gargantuan step of selling their old residence in a remote part of the Rocky Mountains and had moved herself, her mentally and physically dependent husband, and all their household goods to a major city and medical hub where she could get good medical care for him and emotional support for herself. They lived, temporarily, in a small apartment, while she looked for an affordable condo. Still, she could scarcely get away for anything. She was now at the point of having groceries delivered, along with virtually everything else she needed. Going to any kind of store or business with Phil was impossible.

She and I had agreed upon a telephone call today, and we hoped for enough time. Our agenda was to identify what assets were now owned after all the shuffle from the move. Barbara had complained that she still was having a difficult time identifying anything meaningful when she looked at the brokerage account statements. And as money was coming in from the sale of the house and various household items and going out for rent and furnishing the new apartment, she didn't know which account to use for what. Her answer to the dilemma was to open new accounts. Barbara named five different banks and credit unions where she held savings, money market accounts; and CDs. She also whispered that she had a stash of $100 bills in her dresser and a small box of gold coins that Phil had bought a few years ago. There also were IRAs and stock accounts that were held at a brokerage firm.

I briefly described four categories of assets and asked Barbara to identify which of her assets belonged in each category.

"Well, I know the IRAs and stock accounts would go in #2, Financial Investments. And the $100 bills go in #1. Cash. But I'm not sure about the rest."

"Okay, that's a good start," I responded.

Barbara was surprised to learn that all of her savings, money market accounts, bills, and CDs were categorized in the first category: Cash. I explained it this way, "Cash is a category for anything you own that holds no discernible *risk* and is *liquid*. In other words, it can be changed to an equivalent cash amount anytime. That is true of checking accounts, savings accounts, money market funds and CDs. Yes, the CDs have a maturity date and a penalty if you cash them out early, but you have a ready market for converting them – your bank – and essentially you can do that anytime the bank is open."

## To Risk or Not to Risk

There is a tradeoff for having money *liquid*, *i.e.*, easily accessible. In order to have that convenience, you get paid a much lower interest rate on your money. In other words, the risk is low, but so is the return.

"In contrast," I continued with Barbara, "think about the real estate you just sold. It took quite a bit of time to find the buyer. You couldn't just go to the real estate firm and say, 'I'd like my money.' Right? And you didn't know exactly how much money you would get for the house, once you found a possible buyer. No one guaranteed a price, so there was some risk."

"The same is true of the IRAs and stock accounts," I explained. "You don't have an exact figure of what any of them will be worth when you are ready to sell. And you will have to sell them on the open stock exchange. There is no guarantee what the investments will be worth. But you hope you will have made more in these accounts than you could have in the money markets. Hopefully, you will. In other words, there is more risk but potentially more reward."

Barbara thought she was providing a great deal of safety for her money by having it all in cash. Her circumstances made this totally understandable. But her strategy for safety was completely eliminating the possibility of higher reward. In fact, she was risking running out of money. The higher reward is a necessary component for all money that will be invested for greater than 3 years. If you are unwilling to take this additional risk, you must accept the certainty that taxes and inflation will eat into your investment.

## Cash

You need liquid assets because you need money ready for emergencies. You also need money in cash assets if you are planning to spend that money in three years or less. Everyone needs liquid money stashed away for the emergencies in life, the unexpected events that spawn a need for cash quickly. An emergency fund is for those real needs we have, the Essentials that are not in the budget because they are not predictable as to time and amount of need. Things like the roof that suddenly has a leak, the refrigerator that goes out, or an out-of-pocket expense for a hospital visit. Emergency funds keep us from having to use credit when life happens. You are prepared for the unexpected life. You are the squirrel in autumn, caching extra nuts before winter.

How much is enough? As with most situations, the answer is, "It depends." Most people keep too little: they are spending too much and depending on credit for emergencies. Others keep way too much because they feel insecure about their money management. Here are my recommendations:

- If you are a two-income family with fairly secure jobs, then three months of your expenses in a liquid account will do it. For example -

  If your Total Expenses are $80,000 per year, (divide by 12 months and multiply by 3 months) you should have roughly $20,000 in a savings account or in a money market.

- If you are single (or you are married but incomes are not very secure) a reserve of six months of your Total Expenses is best for you.

  (Divide your annual expenses by 12 and multiply by 6.)

- You should also have a **Spending Fund** for annual payments that are due. Keeping a total of one year's annual payments is the best plan.

- Cash in Retirement. If you are retired, things are a bit different.

  In this situation, I prefer to use the reserve **Spending Fund** for your annual spending. No need for an

Emergency Fund, since there is no job to lose, and you are already including in your budget items like extra medical expenses, house repairs, and new car purchase. Your **Spending Fund** should equal 1-3 years of Non-Essential Spending *if* you have a guaranteed income source for your Essential Spending. If you don't have enough guaranteed income, then your Total Expenses minus whatever guaranteed income you do have (multiplied by 1-3 years) should be in your Spending Fund.

## Other Cash Needs: Short-Term Savings

Besides Emergency Funds or Spending Funds, the second need for cash is a savings account for any expenses not in the budget that are certain to come up. If you know some expenses will be coming up within a three-year time frame, you need a cash account to pay for them. This could be a down payment for a house, college expenses, replacing a car, *etc*. For example, Barbara intended to purchase a new condo within a year. She also needed moving expenses, and perhaps some new items for the house. She estimated the cost to be $250,000. We designated a separate account for this expenditure.

The lesson is that if you anticipate a need in less than three years, it should not be invested in the stock market or in bonds. You must be willing to give up potential growth in order to have liquidity and surety. It is a necessary trade-off. If you expect to need the money in five years, for example, you might put 3/5 of the money in a money market account and 2/5 in stable investments in the stock market.

(Note that savings accounts and money markets are used interchangeably. Just find whichever has better interest rates and is convenient to you.)

Let's turn back to Barbara. After the sale of her home, 2nd car, and tools and farm equipment, her Success Matrix assets looked like this:

## Exhibit 5: Barbara's Current Situation

| Gross Income | | Expenses | | Cash Flow |
|---|---|---|---|---|
| Total Guaranteed Income | $36,000 | Essential spending | $34,400 | |
| Social security: $28,000 | | Non-Essential Lifestyle | 15,000 | |
| Annuity: $8,000 | | Debt Payments | | |
| Total Other Income | 17,600 | Credit Card | 2,400 | |
| | | Income Taxes | 1,200 | |
| Total Income | $53,600 | Total Expenses | $53,000 | Cash Flow    $600 |

| Assets | | Liabilities | | Net Worth |
|---|---|---|---|---|
| Cash in checking Acct | $469,000 | Credit Cards | $5,000 | |
| Emergency Savings | 0 | | | |
| Savings Accts& Gold | 465,000 | | | |
| Financial Investments | 40,000 | | | |
| Home | 0 | Mortgage | 0 | |
| Car | 15,000 | Car | 0 | |
| Total Assets | $989,000 | Total Liabilities | $5,000 | Net Worth    $984,000 |

- Barbara and Phil are retired. Their guaranteed income from Social Security and an annuity provide about the same amount she has for Essential Needs. Perfect!

- She needs to cover Non-Essential Spending and Tax expenses ($17,500 per year) from her Assets each year. Financial Investments are a tiny portion of her total assets, and yet, will need to supply the $17,500 each year to provide the funds for those expenses.

- You can see that cash assets in the checking and savings accounts are more than 90% of the assets! We need to reallocate as much of her cash as possible to stock investments so that she can experience growth in order to cover her expenses.

This is how I changed her allocation:

## Exhibit 6: Barbara's New Allocation of Cash

| Gross Income | | Expenses | | Cash Flow |
|---|---|---|---|---|
| Total Guaranteed Income | $36,000 | Essential spending | $34,400 | |
| Social security: $28,000 | | Non-Essential Lifestyle | 15,000 | |
| Annuity: $8,000 | - | Debt Payments | | |
| Total Other Income | 17,600 | Credit Card | 0 | |
| | | Income Taxes | 1,200 | |
| **Total Income** | **$53,600.00** | **Total Expenses** | **$50,600** | **Cash Flow**    **$3,000** |

| Assets | | Liabilities | | Net Worth |
|---|---|---|---|---|
| Cash in checking Acct | $5,000 | Credit Cards | $0 | |
| Spending Account | 17,500 | | | |
| Savings for House | 250,000 | | | |
| Financial Investments | $656,500 | | | |
| Gold coins | 40,000 | | | |
| Home | 0 | Mortgage | 0 | |
| Car | 15,000 | Car | 0 | |
| **Total Assets** | **$984,000** | **Total Liabilities** | **$0** | **Net Worth**    **$984,000** |

- The first thing we did was eliminate her $5,000 credit card debt. That was just too silly, given the fact that she had loads of cash. Saving that $2400/credit card payment was a relief to Barbara, and improved her cash flow.

- We separated enough cash to supply Barbara's need for Spending Funds for one year.

- We also kept money in Money Market for the upcoming condo purchase and move.

- Once the cash asset needs were satisfied, everything else was invested in Financial Assets for more growth.

Cash is quite an important asset class. It keeps us safe and secure. But keeping too much in savings will keep us poor. Interestingly, Barbara's lack of understanding this truth let her to use credit, which worsened her cash flow and her financial security considerably.

Now let's explore the other categories of assets.

## Financial Investments

If you are storing up money for things you may need, not this year or the next, but in five, ten, or twenty years, it is appropriate and wise to look to financial investments. Typical accounts in this category are your retirement savings and your after-tax savings that you might have with a brokerage firm for longer-term goals. The investments we are speaking of are generally regulated by the SEC: stocks, bonds, mutual funds, variable annuities, Exchange Traded Funds (ETFs), or options. These are usually liquid, but they have values that fluctuate, depending on the stock market or bonds in which they are invested.

However, because you have more than a three-year time horizon, you have a good chance of being rewarded for the risk you have taken. Accepting more risk will likely give more growth on an asset, if given enough time. You want to surpass the rate of inflation, and looking for 5%-10% average annual return is reasonable. You must accept the potential that some years will deliver a negative return. But averaged over five (5) or ten (10) years, your 10% average return will far surpass the savings account rate plus inflation and taxes.

There are countless books and articles on how to invest and where to invest. I encourage you to read and learn more. That is not my mission in this book. Money management is my goal. There are three essential tenets to managing your investments:

**First is *Diversification*.** This is by far, the most impactful thing you can do to make your money safer. The narrower your bet, the more you are at risk. If you invest in one individual stock, you have only one chance to win. That company has to succeed or you lose. If you invest in a managed mutual fund, you have a pool of stock or bond picks. That has less risk. But if you buy an index, you are buying an entire category of stocks or bonds, and your risk is spread even more. So, diversification of asset classes, of sectors and countries is all important.

**Next is *Costs*.** There are costs for advice and there are costs for the investments themselves (in commissions or expense ratios), that can syphon off your profits. If your investments are doing great, but year after year, you are paying a lot for your guidance, well...your bucket has a hole in it. Right?

**The third element is *Ongoing Management.*** If you are invested in securities, there is no "set it and forget it." You must make sure your exposure to market risk is appropriate to your changing age, goals, and markets. You may choose a "robo" investment plan. That means that an online tool helps you decide how to invest, where to invest, and makes the trades for you. Through the years, it should also keep rebalancing the portfolio automatically to adjust to your age, goals, and changing markets. There is no advisor to call, but there are resources online that can help you if you need it. If you are an accumulator, and not a retiree, this *may* be a perfect solution for you.

On the other hand, if you are retired, or you simply need to have a conversation with a real person – maybe you have more complex issues in your life – then you will want an advisor. That will add to your cost, but they will stay on top of changing the portfolio as you age or your goals change. The costs are calculated on the total dollars they manage. (Tip: Your advisor should manage *all* your assets so you have a cohesive plan. Don't try to scrimp here.) Fees can range from 0.25% to 1.50% per year of the value of your portfolio. Choose wisely. That is a wide range of possible fees.

I encourage you to find an advisor or a broker dealer whom you trust and let them guide you either with a "robo" app or a live advisor. I have listed several good resources in the Resource section of the book for places to start your search.

## Real Estate

Real Estate is usually considered your least liquid asset. It may take months, even years to find a buyer for the price you want. National averages of growth in value hover at 4% per year.

The value of your real estate is the Fair Market Value or what the selling price may be in today's market. You can use Zillow (they say their estimates are within 10% of the selling price of the home), or your realtor or an appraiser (for a fee) to get this value. That valuation is the number to list in your Assets Column. (The mortgage is listed in the Liability section. See the Debt chapter for a review of this.) To calculate your equity, take your Fair Market Value and subtract the mortgage. For instance, if in today's market, you think you could sell your house for $500,000 and you owe $200,000, then your equity is $300,000. If you own an investment property, include it in your Assets also. If the property produces income, include the annual rent in your total income.

Real Estate is non-correlated to the stock market. That means real estate doesn't normally make moves at the same time or in the same direction as the market. The Great Recession of 2008 was an exception to that rule. Since the major cause of the recession was irresponsible lending that created a mortgage credit crunch and a mortgage bubble, both real estate and stock market prices took a major hit in the same time sequence. That said, they don't *normally* move in tandem. Therefore, buying real estate is a good hedge or diversification to the stock market. It's good to own both.

## Hard Assets

What are hard assets? As opposed to financial assets, which are only recorded on paper, hard assets can be touched and seen. Hard assets have special challenges and considerations, like storage and finding specialty buyers. This category includes items like jewelry, precious metals (gold or silver coins or bullion), art, collectibles, and rare or antique vehicles.

Hard assets are often very illiquid. You have to find the right buyer who values the item like you do. You may need to find a specialty auction. And the asset may go in and out of favor or popularity, which affects the value. Just watch "Antiques Roadshow" on PBS to get an idea of these types of assets. You must become an expert on the particular assets to really know the value of what you are collecting and who your potential market is. Also, there is a cost to owning them because you must insure the items. They are subject to ruin from the elements or thievery or fire. I would never suggest sinking your hard-earned savings into hard assets if you don't have a love and passion about the items you are collecting.

I have an example in my own family of someone who successfully managed this. My dearly loved aunt was widowed and left with only the house she lived in and a small Social Security income. She had not worked outside the home, and had very limited earning potential. But she looked around at what she *did* have. She had a drawer of antique silver spoons which she had collected at flea markets over the years. In fact, she had quite a stash of them! And she had a collection of antique dolls. She studied the markets that bought and sold these items. Over the years, she supported herself quite nicely. When she died, she had some impressive savings in her bank account! Making money with hard assets can be done, if you are willing to become knowledgeable and have the mindset of a smart trader.

Everything you own contributes to your net worth. Make sure all the asset classes you own are entered in your Workbook Asset worksheets. It all counts. We'll see how in the new chapter.

Purchase the Hidden Figures Workbook here: www.MyHiddenFigures.net

# NET WORTH

## Meaning of Money

*M*oney is a thing. Like food and dirt, buildings and cars, it is just a material thing in this material world. It doesn't have intrinsic meaning. It only has the meaning we give it.

Some people think money is an indicator of worth. They subconsciously declare that it measures approval from the gods. They act like the possession of a lot of money proves superiority.

The opposite opinion also exists. Some think financial hard times equate to unworthiness. They believe those who have less *are* less. Maybe the gods have cursed them.

Hidden Figure #7 is Net Worth. Not *Your* Worth. It pulls together all the other Hidden Figures to give an accurate picture of your financial reality. Keep this number in reality, not in projected meaning.

Your Net Worth is a number to watch year after year to see the trajectory of your financial life, and the safety of your financial position. It is the bottom line of your *financial* success. The equation for finding your Net Worth is as simple as the equation for Cash Flow: Assets – Liabilities = Net Worth.

Mary, Barbara, and Joanne have each had a year to work on Net Worth. Of course, the process for them was like it has been for you. Each had to analyze and list her income. They listed and evaluated their every expense. They entered all liabilities and the corresponding expenses. They examined their own tax forms and estimated their Taxes, then categorized their Assets. They examined their Cash Flow and Net Worth. In other words, they found all of their Hidden Figures and entered them into the Success Matrix.

Just like you. Now, looking at your Success Matrix, you can see your Net Worth. Whether it is horrifying or exhilarating, you know what it is. Knowing your Net Worth is the culmination of all your work thus far. And now you can decide what to do about it.

## Why is Net Worth so important?

I can think of three major reasons Net Worth is important:

## 1. It Supports Your Why

Do you want to spend a year abroad? Do you want to give a year of your life helping a charity? Do you want to help your niece or grandson through college? Do you want to buy a cottage on the beach? What do you want to do? Where do you want to be? What life goals and dreams do you want to fulfill? With a significant net worth, the choice is yours. Freedom. That's what net worth brings.

*Why* would you like to grow your Net Worth? It helps to know your why. As you journal this week, you can explore this question.

Net Worth is ideally growing every year. You judge your financial decisions by whether your net worth will increase or decrease. If you are growing in net worth every year, then you are increasing your chances of weathering a big storm in your life (and we all have them). You are also increasing the freedom of choices in your life. Think of it: with higher Net Worth, in good times, you have more freedom, in bad times, you are still standing.

I had a friend who often said, "Money can't solve all your problems. But I can't think of one that money wouldn't make it better." I always laughed. It's not just that you can throw cash at a problem and it goes away. If your finances are in order, and you have, not only income, but assets without debt hanging over your head, you have a multitude of choices at your fingertips.

## 2. It Helps You Make Your Own Decisions

Don't get me wrong. I am a big believer in getting counsel, advice and/or coaching. But that is not the same as leaving the decision up to someone else. You must be able to bring an informed question and opinion to your trusted advisors. Then their advice means something for *your* situation. You will spot it if you are being given generic advice – one size does **not** fit all. You can intelligently analyze their response based on your life and present circumstances. You also know and accept the fact that no one knows or cares more about your Net Worth or situation than you do.

**Depending on someone else to make your financial
decisions is like getting into a taxi and asking,
"Where do you think I should go?"**

### 3. It Allows You to Live in the Moment While
### Building a Future

"I just want to live in the moment," groaned Joanne. We were
discussing Net Worth and how it should be growing each year.
"I just lost my husband. I'm tired of putting things off for the
future. I want to live right now."

She voiced an excellent point. We *should* be living right
now. We *should* be living in the moment. Living in the moment
means doing your very best right now, using all your senses
to take in, enjoy and figure out right now; not tomorrow,
but now. It means you are using all your mental, physical,
and financial resources to contribute all you are, here on this
earth, to contribute. You are bringing your very best and
offering it to everything you do. You are taking responsibility
for how you spend your limited resources. (All resources are
finite, right?) You are treating it with respect, thinking clearly
about each asset's best use and how it can help you live your
best life.

On the other hand, living *for* the moment simply says
that financial reality is not important. "Oh, what the hell.
I need a vacation!" might be a justification for disregarding
responsibilities. It says that you can blow things off, even disregarding commitments and financial safety. I am not saying
that any spontaneous expenditure is a bad idea. But I am
talking about justifying poor financial decisions. There is a

huge difference in living *in* the moment as opposed to living *for* the moment. We bring about our very best life when we live respectfully with what we've been given. That's living *in* the moment.

## Interconnectedness Of All The Quadrants

Your online Success Matrix has two different "What-if" scenarios. You have now completed the Current Scenario. But if you want, you can play with the figures by comparing two different financial choices with the "What-If" tools. You will see that all four quadrants – Income, Expenses, Assets, and Liabilities – are interconnected. The Cash Flow and Net Worth reflect any changes you make in the quadrants. Let's explore how they work together.

### Income and Cash Flow

Your sources of income are juxtaposed with your categories of expenses. If you have an income increase, you will more than likely have an increase in taxes. Yet, overall, your Cash Flow will be up. Increased Cash Flow means you can add to your Investments/Savings or reduce your Liabilities. Of course, you can choose to do neither and spend the cash flow. But if you want to increase your Net Worth, then increasing Assets or decreasing Liabilities is the way to go. You are increasing your Net Worth and adding to your safety by either of those two choices.

Note: if you are spending your cash flow, then you should increase your expense number to show that you actually *don't* have cash flow.

## Liabilities

Remember: you must enter your debts on two lines: there is the liability (the entire amount you owe to the bank or credit card company or mortgage company) and there is the payment for that debt. One is entered in the Liability quadrant and the other is entered in the Expense quadrant. A liability decreases *both* your Cash Flow and your Net Worth. And decreasing your liabilities increases both Cash Flow and Net Worth.

I developed this Matrix to help you see the connectedness of every financial decision and how it will impact both your Cash Flow and your Net Worth. Usually, I found that my clients were weak in only one or two of the quadrants. They were weak in income, but had adequate assets. Or their spending was way out of whack, not allowing them to save enough. Most of the time, it would only take an adjustment in one or two habits to find the balance. Seeing how each quadrant affects the other is a major step forward in being able to create financial stability.

## What if? Negative Cash Flow

When you are living with a negative Cash Flow, you are either spending your Assets or you are adding to your Liabilities. Of course, as noted above, if you are adding to your liabilities, then your expenses are going up as well, which increases the negative Cash Flow. Use your "What If" scenarios to play with this. Keep spending in one scenario and in a second scenario, decrease spending enough to eliminate the negative cash flow. Or increase Income to eliminate negative cash flow. Do some projecting with the values for next year, with either scenario. Find out if Net Worth will increase or decrease.

## What if? Positive Cash Flow

Now start a new "What If" scenario to see what happens when you have a positive cash flow.

Use the example of spending that extra money. Obviously, if you spent on a new wardrobe, the money is gone and there is nothing to add to the Success Matrix but an expense.

But you could remodel your kitchen. The money is still spent. Does it change anything else? Think through each quadrant and ask yourself if anything changes. I can think of a few changes this spending would generate.

Maybe your expenses would go down because you would cook at home more, or entertain at home more. If expenses stay down, then next year's Cash Flow increases more. Now, maybe you save more. Maybe the value of your home would increase with the new kitchen. In either or both of these cases, your Net Worth increases because of positive changes in Expenses and Assets.

On the other hand, what if you take out a loan for this remodel? Again, consider all four quadrants. Do your expenses go up or down? The value of the home may go up, so you could increase the home value in Assets. But the loan adds to the Liabilities. Play with some specific numbers to see what happens to the Net Worth and Cash Flow. Then make your best guess as to where the values would be in the next year.

I hope this is a big eye-opener – to see how every financial decision has long-term effects in all four quadrants of your Success Matrix, and ultimately, in your Net Worth. I am encouraging you to use this tool extensively and thoughtfully before you make decisions. Look at, not only the immediate effect, but consider what the effect will be in one, two, or three years.

My prayer for you is that you can accept that money is just a *thing*. Not a good thing, not a bad thing. Just a thing. It is up to you to use it in a good way, a way that brings joy to your life and others. Knowing your Hidden Figures will help you do this.

## Bonus "What-If" Scenario

Buying an investment property is a much more complicated analysis. If you are up to it, let's use a "What If" scenario to dig deeper.

Scenario 1 takes more out of savings to make a larger down payment. Scenario 2 leaves more in savings, but takes on a bigger loan.

## Scenario 1

Here are the facts: Market Value of the house is $350,000. You have $100,000 in Financial Assets. You want to make a down payment of $50,000. Your mortgage is $300,000. And your monthly debt payment is $1,500. Let's assume you currently have a positive cash flow of $18,000 ($1,500/month). In this case, you can afford the payment.

- Enter $118,000 as income and $50,000 in *each* – Essential expense and Non-Essential Expense – just for illustration.
- Now add $18,000 in debt expense. Enter $350,000 in assets.

- Enter $50,000 left in Financial Investments.
- Enter $300,000 in Liabilities.

Your Cash Flow should be $0. And your Net Worth is $100,000.

## Scenario 2

Now we ask the question: Since you have $100,000 in Financial Assets, what if you put more into a down payment? All other facts remain the same. You put $60,000 down and your loan is now $290,000. Your mortgage payment equals $16,000. Look at all 4 quadrants to see what changes should be made.

- No change to income
- Change the mortgage payment to $16,000
- Change the Financial Investment to $40,000
- No change to value of home
- Change loan to $290 000

What do you see? For one, there is better Cash Flow. Now you have $2,000 more each year. Where could that money go? Could you pay down the loan faster? Could you add money back to your brokerage account? What will your Net Worth likely be in a year?

You also see that your Net Worth has not changed. You gave up an extra $10,000 in your Financial Investments for $10,000 additional equity in the investment property. Will your positive Cash Flow influence your Net Worth in years to come? You bet it will!

Feel free to explore your own possibilities in the "What If" Success Matrix. Blank pages are printed in the Workbook and they are also available online.

Purchase the workbook here: www. MyHiddenFigures.net

# PART II

# PULLING IT ALL TOGETHER

ou've uncovered your previously Hidden Figures. You've given them a hard look and made some decisions. Now it's time to plan for the rest of your life. Because of your discoveries, there is a new way of life! There is a purpose in the way you handle your money. Hopefully, there is a great deal less fear and a lot more confidence.

Part II, Pulling It Together, will show you how to make this an ongoing way of life. You can keep this upward momentum of taking control of your finances. Like anything, once you build a habit, it becomes second nature and the effort is minimal. I will show you what habits are important.

Your financial notebook will be put to ongoing use. You can continue to use your journaling page in the Workbook. Once they are used, you can start fresh with a new three-ring binder. Your notebook will need three sections: Journal Section, Budget/Money Meeting Section, and Annual Hidden Figures Meeting. I'll give details on how to use your notebook in each of the habits.

## Habit 1: Set up, Budget, and Monitor Your Finances

First you must create a budget – a Spending Plan. Your Success Matrix is the place where decisions are made. Once you see how much you need to spend, save, or cut back, you can make your spending plan, that reflects your decisions. The budget will be a document of your intentions. Your intentions are based on your values, your goals and your newly adopted principles of financial management. Just remember the Success Matrix is your sounding board for all you need to do and all you want to do. Don't lapse back into emotional financial management.

Your Spending Plan declares how you **want** to use your money. You can use an electronic app or go old school and monitor it by hand. If you are going electronic, you will connect your bank, brokerage accounts, loans, and credit card feeds to the app so it can collect your every expenditure. I use Quicken to collect all my expenditures. There are many apps available and you can choose what is comfortable for you. Check the Resource page for a starting point.

Once the app is set up, you will compare your expenditures with your Spending Plan. Notice where you need to make corrections. Make a plan on how you will correct course if you veer off course. Most importantly, get agreement with all in your household to work together on this agreement.

How often should this happen? I have done this for so long, I only check the reports once a month. It takes a quick look to see if any expenditures were miscoded. Then I print a report that compares my Expense categories with my Budget. I see if I have overspent and need to correct. My husband and I ask ourselves a series of questions, make our agreements and plans. Then we are done with our monthly Money Meeting.

If you are new to this, you can have this meeting weekly. Maybe a family meeting is appropriate if you have others living with you who also have financial responsibilities. If handling finances is completely new and you are unsteady, I would approach this much like you would a new diet. You must write down everything you spend **every day** (like writing down every bite of food that goes in your mouth). You must analyze your expenditures and compare them to your plan until you can stay on course and make financial decisions without having to refer to your plan on every item.

In your binder, make a "Budget/Money Meeting" section. Each time my Money Meeting occurs (daily, weekly, monthly), I add two pages to my binder. I include a copy of the report from my Quicken file. It shows a chart of my actual spending compared to my spending plan. I also print a Word document that asks these four questions and has space for me to write the answers. When the page is filled out with my answers, it goes in my binder with the Spending Plan report. There is a printable PDF online at www.MyHiddenFigures.net Here are the four questions:

1. What are my "wins" for this spending period? What did I do well? What did I accomplish?
2. What were my "un-accomplishments"? What do I wish I had done better? What didn't work? What did I not attempt that I wanted to accomplish?
3. What got in my way? What held me back? What did I say to myself? What did I learn?
4. What do I want the next Money Meeting to look like? What are my next steps? What are my non-negotiables for next time – things I am committed to doing no matter what?

## Habit 2: Set Your Three-year Goals

The next habit to build is to have an Annual Hidden Figures meeting. In preparation for this meeting you must set your three-year goals. I learned this from some executive training from Franklin Planners. In these trainings they talked about five-year goals. Stephen Covey's *The Seven Habits of Highly Effective People*[5] was the basis of their training. I gained so much from this training, but I came to believe that in our fast-paced world, five years was too far out. Who knows what will happen in five years? Goals get too nebulous in that range. I pulled it back to three years and discovered that, in my own planning, I am better able to envision what I want my future to be within that time frame.

One of the main concepts Covey taught was to "Start with the End in Mind." Every year, you should make plans for the coming three years. Where is your life headed? Find the Treasure Map assignment in the Workbook Journal Prompts. Make your own Treasure Map and use this for a starting place of your three year goals. Also review your journals from Hidden Figure #7 where you dreamed about a life with a growing Net Worth. These brainstorms and soul searches will be the basis for your three-year plan. From there, fill in the blanks below. Give yourself as much room to write as you want. And write it out as many different times as it takes until you are happy. Then add this to your Money Binder, behind the Annual Meeting tab. You may print a downloadable PDF version of the 3-year Goals from the website www.MyHiddenFigures.net.

---

[5] S. Covey, *The Seven Habits of Highly Effective People*, Free Press, New York, NY (1989).

## GOAL PLANNER

### In Three Years

**Goal 1:** I want to be, have, go, or experience -

With whom?

By what dates?

Why?

**Goal 2:** I want to be, have, go, or experience

With whom?

_____

_____

By what dates?

_____

_____

Why?

_____

_____

**You may have as many goals as you want. The printable version will have 5.**

### Habit 3: Hidden Figures Annual Meeting

Now for the culmination of it all! Set aside some time to plan the *big picture* for each year. If you can arrange a long weekend or even a week away from the house, it is ideal. Borrow or rent a cabin, stay with a friend who will give you time alone, use a time-share to get away. Book a local hotel that is running a special. Or stay at home, but purchase ready-to-eat meals and turn off phones and computers. Do whatever it takes to maximize the efficiency of your time and focus. Find time to play and relax, but also have some serious discussions or brainstorm sessions to review your total financial picture. Sounds fun, doesn't it? It really is. Go ahead. You deserve this. Plan to do this one year from now. Or choose a different time of the year, but keep it annual from there. November works well for the tax planning issues. But you decide. Where will you go? Should anyone be with you? Put it on the calendar *and in the budget.*

Here are the items you need to prepare in advance.

1. Enter current numbers into your online Success Matrix and print.

2. Get copies of your most recent tax returns. You might look ahead at the questions regarding taxes and have a conversation with your tax advisor ahead of your planning meeting.

3. Gather documents needed to show your income for the last 12 months (end-of-year paycheck stub, or Balance Sheet for your business, etc.).

4. Bring your Money Notebook with notes from your **Money Meetings** and your **three-year goals**.

## Annual Meeting Agenda

1. Begin with the End in Mind!

   **a. Review your three-year Goals**. Mark off any items that have already been achieved and celebrate those achievements!

   b. Have you changed your opinion about some goals? Edit the list!

2. **Review your latest Net Worth**.

   a. Compare your updated Success Matrix with your previous Success Matrix.

   b. Note your progress or lack thereof.

**3. Review your Income and Tax status**. November is often an ideal time because you have some idea of how the year's earnings have gone for the current year. And the previous year's tax return has been filed. Here are some questions to ask yourself and/or your tax advisor:

a. Was this year's income higher than normal?

b. Will you be in a higher income tax bracket than last year?

   i. Can you contribute more to charities to bring your income down?

   ii. Would additional contributions lower your highest tax bracket?

c. Or was your income lower than usual?

   i. Are there some selling opportunities to take advantage of because of lower capital gains tax rates?

b. Did you have enough taxes deducted or withheld? Or will you likely have to pay more in April?

c. And what about the coming year? Are your earnings on a big upward trajectory that says next year, I'll be paying more taxes than this year? Or can I see that my income, and therefore my taxes, will be less next year? Those are all important facts to consider.

   i. Maybe adjust your withholding?

   ii. Perhaps increase or decrease your retirement plan contributions?

   iii. Should you adjust your gifts to charity?

4. Make a list of the **five things you hold dearest in life.** Make this list anew each year. Could someone else guess this list by seeing how you spend your money? Review your Spending Plan and your Expenses for the year. Are there adjustments you should – and want – to make?

a. Enter those changes to your Spending Plan, either online or in your paper copy.

b. Keep your list and the changes in your **Annual Meeting Notes**.

5. Answer the **Coaching Questions** from your **Money Meetings** again, this time with your whole year in mind. Also, refer back to your **three-year goals** and plan your steps toward those goals.

a. What are my "wins" for this spending period? What did I do well? What did I accomplish?

b. What were my "un-accomplishments"? What do I wish I had done better? What did not work? What did I not attempt that I wanted to accomplish?

c. What got in my way? What held me back? What did I say to myself? What did I learn?

d. What do I want my next Money Meeting to look like? What are my next steps? What are my non-negotiables for next time – things I am committed to doing no matter what?

6. **Transfer your specific commitments to a calendar**.

a. If you are doing this planning with another household member, decide who is responsible for what tasks.

b. This is not a time to discuss faults or mistakes, other than to see where you could make things better. This is a time to look at *what is* and to *find solutions* for things you want to change. Discover what you want and find viable options for how to get there.

c. Always look for a way to give safety to your plans through alternate plans. Remember Plan A and Plan B from the Hidden Figure #3 Debt.

Note: Always add your notes to your Money Binder with this year's date. And mark your calendar for next year's meeting!

Each of these six steps should take about 60-90 minutes. I think they work best if kept in order. If you have a long weekend, you might plan for Steps 1 and 2 the first day, Steps 3 and 4 the second day, and Steps 5 and 6 the third day. Perhaps you would schedule one meeting after breakfast and the second after lunch for each day. If you have a whole week, you can choose the same time each day to knock out one step.

This Annual Meeting agenda is available in printable PDF online at www.MyHiddenFigures.net

## Looking Back

Right now, you can't imagine how much progress you will make if you commit to this meeting year after year. It can be the lifeblood of your ongoing progress. Each of these figures represents a huge part of your financial life. Just think of it.

**Income** represents your contribution to a for-profit or philanthropic endeavor. Hopefully, it is meaningful and enjoyable for you. There is always room for honest evaluation about whether you are giving your best and whether you are receiving what you deserve.

**Spending** says so much about you. Are you tied to material things? Are you hoarding or pinching every last penny? You've moved through lots of evaluation of your Essential Spending and your Non-Essential Spending. Hard work! And every last ounce of effort will be worth it. This step requires the very most ongoing effort. I know you are up to the task.

**Debt** evaluations are perhaps the hardest. Now you have it in black and white. How much do you owe and what is it costing you in monthly bills? You've put together a plan to move that debt to something manageable or get it out of your life altogether. It feels good, doesn't it?

**Taxes** are a slog for most. But now you are equipped with new knowledge and tools to maximize that hard-earned income! It has to feel good to have a better handle on how taxes are calculated and how yours stacks up on the scale.

**Assets** could be the high point of putting all this together. At least it is likely the easiest assignment. Now, seeing it in its place on the Success Matrix, you can evaluate its value to you more clearly. Your goal is much clearer, isn't it?

**Cash Flow and Net Worth** are the calculations done for you. They are the eye-openers that help you see what needs to happen with the other Figures. From these, you can adjust your plans, set your goals and make sense of your financial position.

Make sure all worksheets and Journal Prompts have been completed in your *Hidden Figures Workbook*. Purchase the workbook here: www.MyHiddenFigures.net

That's it! You have uncovered Seven Hidden Figures that have brought clarity and focus to your financial life. I believe with these tools and concepts, you will manage your money with more ease, more confidence and a lot more safety! I hope it has been a rewarding journey for you.

Blessings!

\*      \*      \*

If you would like more coaching and support for these steps, please visit my website for upcoming Online Hidden Figures Classes and/or Live Coaching. www.MyHiddenFigures.net/Books and Courses

\*      \*      \*

# RESOURCES

## Recommended Reading

- *ALLIE AND BEA* - novel by Catherine Ryan Hyde
- *THE MILLIONAIRE NEXT DOOR* by Thomas J. Stanley
- *THE RICHEST MAN IN BABYLON* by George S. Clason
- *RICH DAD POOR DAD* by Robert Kiyosaki & Sharon Lechter
- *THE TOTAL MONEY MAKEOVER* by Dave Ramsey
- *THE LITTLE BOOK OF COMMON SENSE INVESTING: THE ONLY WAY TO GUARANTEE YOUR FAIR SHARE OF STOCK MARKET RETURNS* by John C. Bogle
- *THE MORE OF LESS: FINDING THE LIFE YOU WANT UNDER EVERYTHING YOU OWN* by Joshua Becker

## Digital Budgeting Tools

- Mint.com
- Quicken.com
- Quickbooks.com (for self-employed)
- Mvelopes.com
- Your Own bank's app or resource

# ACKNOWLEDGEMENTS

There is no doubt that this book would never have been written without the consistent encouragement and support given to me by my husband, Michael. He is and always will be my biggest fan.

And my clients have bolstered me in ways I cannot express. They have inspired me, niggled my conscious, kept me awake at night searching for solutions for them, their families and their daunting situations. They have inspired me and taught me and made me do better. I love them for their courage and tenacity.

Extreme appreciation for all the professionals who have helped me. My editor, Kelly Lydick was great to work with and my second editor, Michael, searched for syntax, verb agreement and general making sense. Fabulous job from both. My coach, Erin Tamberella, pushed and prodded me to keep my promised schedule. She also encouraged me about my writing at a time when I felt so vulnerable. Tim, my cover designer, was fun to work with, and he amazed me with his creativity and understanding of what I wanted. Amit Dey, formatted my book perfectly. He was patient and thorough when I was exhausted and couldn't see the end in sight. He signed his emails "With Love" and I loved him for that. Both he and Tim had brand new infants in their homes when they were working with me. I can't imagine how distracted they must have been and yet they did stellar jobs. For all, my gratitude, and humble thanks.

Made in the USA
Monee, IL
16 January 2021